W9-AKC-391

What readers say about *Simplify Your Life*

- Your book is a miracle! This is a significant piece of the pie I have been looking for. Thank you for giving me the additional push I need to get me on my way.

  Sarah Pitkin, Butte, Utah

- The moment I began reading SIMPLIFY YOUR LIFE I loved it! Recently I moved and your book was lost for a few days. Not until I found it did I feel really at home. I hope to be an author some day and I hope my works will be as important to someone as yours are to me.

  Kathy Dempsey, Durham, North Carolina

- Your book is helping me more than I can put into words. Your chapter on downsizing your home was a much-needed validation for me. Now I just need a buyer for my law practice. I'm reading parts of your book every day to get more ideas—some parts I read over and over. I really love the whole thing. What a GREAT work!!

  Sheryl Peterson, Seattle, Washington

- Your book was fun and fast to read, and many of my friends wish to borrow it. Can't let them have it, as I'm still referring to it often, so I guess for $9.95 they can buy their own. Thanks for a great, challenging, thought-provoking book!

  Shirley Reynolds, Diamond Bar, California

- My congratulations to you on a simple, useful, classy book!

  Janice Kimball, Hemet, California

- Your book is a godsend. I'd been praying for years for someone like you. I knew I needed to simplify my life but the usual "Organize Your Stuff" books didn't decrease the density of busyness in my day, just organized it, thereby making the upkeep more complicated. Your book is my bible these days.

  Pamela Crawford, Santa Cruz, California

- Your book has made a world of difference in my life. While reading it I felt like I had a very caring friend talking to me. One way your book has helped me to simplify my life is in gift giving. I bought a bunch of copies and now give them as gifts for every occasion. Thank you for your great work.

  Ellen Looney, New Haven, Connecticut

- I am enjoying your book and have given a dozen or so copies to friends this year. Your message is one whose time has come. Thank you for a very special book.

  David Stearns, Ponte Vedra Beach, Florida

- I loved your book. After I read it I went out and bought five copies for gifts.

  Claire Rich, North Hollywood, California

- Bravo! SIMPLIFY YOUR LIFE is wonderful. I've given copies of it (because I refuse to part with mine) to various friends.

  Ann Hopson, New London, Connecticut

- A therapist friend of mine picked up your book from my coffee table. She loved it and went back to Chicago and bought one for herself and three more for friends. I can tell you every friend of mine is receiving SIMPLIFY YOUR LIFE for their birthday.

  Barbara Carlisle, Freeport, Illinois

- I enjoyed SIMPLIFY YOUR LIFE. It helped me put my life in perspective. My husband and I have been dreaming of buying a bigger house with more storage space, a bigger yard, more rooms, etc, etc. but now I see we're better off than we realized. I suppose we're just a product of a society that trains us to believe bigger is always better and you can never have too much stuff. Thanks for bringing us back to earth.

  Kelli Grady, Ontario, Canada

- From the bottom of my forty-seven-year-old heart I want to thank you (actually, I want to hug you) for writing SIMPLIFY YOUR LIFE. It really spoke to me. It affirmed many of the feelings my wife and I have had for some time.

  Tom Wagner, North Potomac, Maryland

- Thank you for your book. It helped me come a bit closer to Nirvana. I hope you write a second book. By then you'll probably have a cult following. Thanks again for writing the first one.

  Kathy Frederick Louv, San Diego, California

- SIMPLIFY YOUR LIFE is a splendid book and should eliminate most people's need to purchase any further self-help books—that is until SYL-II comes out! Thanks for a great read and many insightful suggestions on making life easier in these crazy times.

  Arlen Bolstad, Richmond, Virginia

SIMPLIFY
YOUR WORK LIFE

ALSO BY ELAINE ST. JAMES

Simplify Your Life

Inner Simplicity

Living the Simple Life

Simplify Your Life with Kids

Simplify Your Christmas

SIMPLIFY

YOUR WORK LIFE

Ways to Change the Way

You Work

So You Have

More Time to Live

ELAINE ST. JAMES

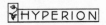

HYPERION

New York

Copyright © 2001 Elaine St. James

All rights reserved. No part of this book may be used or reproduced in any manner whatsoever without the written permission of the Publisher. Printed in the United States of America. For information address: Hyperion, 77 W. 66th Street, New York, New York 10023-6298.

Library of Congress Cataloging-in-Publication Data

St. James, Elaine.
   Simplify your work life : ways to change the way you work so you have more time to live/Elaine St. James.
      p. cm.
   ISBN 0-7868-6683-7
   1. Time management.   2. Organizational effectiveness.   3. Quality of work life. I. Title.
HD69.T54 S725 2001
650.1—dc21   00-061440

Book design by Ruth Lee

FIRST EDITION

10 9 8 7 6 5 4 3 2 1

To
Pat Rushton and Catha Paquette

Here's to another eight years of supporting each other in doing the work we love

CONTENTS

Two: Learning to seize time

Three: Being more productive

Four: Being more effective with people

Contents

INTRODUCTION

A few years back I had a very hectic life and an even more hectic work schedule, the pace of which was probably not all that different from yours. Over the previous fifteen years I managed my own real estate investing business, I ran seminars, and I wrote a book on real estate investing. I got into real estate because I didn't know what else to do, and once I was in I never had the time to figure out how to get out.

Eventually I was working sixty hours a week and was seldom able to spend quality time with my family and friends or even to have time on my own to relax and just putter around the house. I rarely took a vacation and almost never thought about how work had taken over my life.

One day, while looking at my to-do lists, I realized how complicated and out of balance my life had become. I decided right then and there that it was time to simplify. I started by getting rid of a lot of the clutter. I streamlined the cooking, the cleaning, the laundry, and the other household routines; I minimized my wardrobe and drastically changed my consumer habits; and I learned how to say no to the demands on my time.

I also cut back my work schedule. It was a step-by-step process, but by working less I found that I was not only more productive, I also had the time to be more creative and to think about what I wanted to do with my life. Over the next several years I saw that it was time to let go of the real estate business completely. It seemed the height of insanity to spend the majority of my time doing something I didn't truly enjoy.

Then, where people started asking me how I had simplified my life, I took the leap and wrote a book about it. That book, *Simplify Your Life*, became a bestseller. With all the media interviews, the promotional tours, and another book in progress, my work life suddenly had the potential to get complicated all over again. But I was committed to keeping life simple, which I've done. As my writing career developed, I gradually went from my frenetic sixty-hour week to working roughly half that time.

Since then I've come to a new understanding about my life, my work, and my reasons for working. I believed for years that I was working for the money. But I found, as many people have, that money simply isn't reason enough to keep up the grind. I found, as many people are finding, that I'm most productive, most committed, most happy, and most financially rewarded when I love the work I do.

So, contrary to what some may believe, simplifying is not about retreating to a cabin in the woods and leading a dull, inactive existence. Rather, cutting back your hectic work pace gives you the opportunity to make sure that you're doing work you love. If you're not, you can change what you do. Simplifying will also help you create the balance you're seeking in your work life, your family life, and your personal life. Out of that balance you'll have more clarity and enthusiasm to meet your goals. You'll learn how to achieve the success you want without stress and overwork. And simplifying will give you the time to develop a rich and rewarding inner life. Having that inner connection will make it so much easier to move beyond society's demands and expectations about work.

You might have any number of reasons to simplify your work life and any number of goals in mind for doing so.

You may be looking for ways to cut back on the amount of time you work so you'll have time to spend with your family and to do your own puttering around the house. I'll share many ways to free up more time in Parts 1 and 2.

You may love your work but feel that the demands on your time keep you from getting as much done each day as you know you could. In Part 3 I'll show you how to be more productive so you can can cut back on the number of hours you work each week.

You may find that one of the reasons you work so much is that you just can't say no and that inability to set appropriate boundaries keeps you chained to your job. I'll show you some things I've learned about setting boundaries and working effectively with others in Part 4.

You may be intrigued by the idea of simplifying your work life but believe that it's just not possible financially for you to change the way you work. In Part 5 I'll show you how to address the financial issues that may be keeping you locked into a work situation you're not happy with and how to build a new level of financial freedom and security for you and your family.

You may want to restructure your current work by telecommuting, job sharing, arranging a more flexible schedule, or even starting your own business. The opportunities for new ways to work are practically unlimited today. I'll discuss many of these options in Part 6.

You may be tied to outdated ways of thinking about your work and the hours you must spend earning a living, but you should know that there's a whole new world out there now. Just changing the way you think about work will give you a new lease on your work life. You'll find some ways to do that in Part 7.

Though many of the ideas in this book describe office situations, they're relevant for all walks of life. No matter what kind of work you do, you'll find numerous ways to cut back, work more effectively, set appropriate boundaries, become more efficient with your money, and begin to take advantage of the changes that are happening in the workplace.

I invite you to join me in moving with purpose and intention to a simpler work life. This might appear to be a gigantic leap from where you're standing, but once you start the process you'll be able to look back and see that it was really quite a small step. That step is to decide, right now, that you'll do what it takes to keep your work in balance with the rest of your life.

I've been where you are now. I know how challenging it can be to change the way you work. But if I did it—and, as we'll see, thousands of others are doing it—you can, too. Come along with me. Let me show you how you can change the way you work so you have more time to live.

ONE

Cutting Back on

the Amount of Time

You Work

1. Join the Revolution

If you're thinking of cutting back on the amount of time you work, you're not alone. Thousands of American workers are cutting back. After nearly a quarter century of exhausting work schedules, we're coming to our senses and starting to make some changes. A recent Yankelovich poll shows that we're changing how much we work: One in five of us says we've taken a cut in pay to work less. We're changing how we work: Nearly half say we've changed jobs to have more family time. We're changing the way we think about work: Eight out of ten people say we admire someone who puts family before work.

Look around. You probably know people who've cut back their work schedules, who've moved to worker-friendly offices, who've created a more flexible schedule, or who have in one way or another made significant changes in the way they work. Certainly you've read about them. Practically every magazine or newspaper you pick up these days has a story about how people are looking for more balance in their lives and have made the decision to work less. And their numbers are growing every day. The Families and Work Institute reports that in a survey conducted in 1992, 47 percent of the respondents said they wanted to work less; in 1997, 63 percent said they wanted to work less. According to the Trends Research Institute, simplifying will continue to be one of the leading trends of the new millennium.

In addition to the millions of baby boomers who're cutting back, there are millions of GenXers coming into the workplace who've seen their parents burn out working long hours for companies that didn't value their efforts or treated them as a disposable resource. Many of these new workers want to create a more balanced work life than their parents had. I believe there'll soon come a time when our work schedules of the last two decades are seen as a period of temporary cultural insanity.

I invite you to join me and thousands of others in cutting back on the amount of time you work. In this part I'll describe a variety of ways that helped make it possible for me to cut my work schedule from sixty hours a week to roughly thirty. Obviously this didn't happen overnight, and many of the steps I talk about throughout the book helped as well. But freeing up some of the big chunks of time, as I discuss here, is a good place to start.

2. Cut Back to Forty Hours a Week

Whether you love your work, just barely tolerate it, or actively dislike it, the chances are good that you've come to the point where you're ready to work fewer hours, too. So how do you begin?

Start with the realization that it's possible to be happy, productive, fulfilled, and successful working forty hours or less per week. In fact, more and more of us are discovering that the only way to be truly happy, productive, fulfilled, and successful is to cut back on the number of hours we work each week.

Then look at your schedule and make whatever changes are necessary so you can work less. These might include starting your workday later in the morning, leaving the office earlier in the afternoon, limiting or forgoing extended business lunches, not committing to any more grueling projects, or taking any one or more of the steps I outline in Parts 2 and 3 to seize time and be more productive. Become a leader rather than a follower in this regard. Take a quiet stand that says, "I'm good at what I do. I put in my full forty hours, and that's my limit."

As a trial, commit to cutting back to a forty-hour week for the next three to six months. Trust that you're competent enough and capable enough to figure out how to do the things that really need to get done, and don't worry about the rest. Trust that you will gain impetus and fresh insights from the joy of this new beginning.

You may believe it would be impossible to support your lifestyle if you worked less, and at your current rate of consumerism, you might be right. But many people are finding that it's possible to live well on less than they once thought. The solution is so basic: We don't have to work more, we have to spend less (#62).

You might also find, as many people, myself included, have found, that by working less we are free to go beyond the economic limitations set by corporate salary standards. When I simplified my life and cut my work schedule back to forty hours a week, I doubled my income; when I cut my work week to thirty hours, I quintupled it. This seldom happens overnight, but the truth is most people could live well on far less than they're spending if, as we'll see in Part 5, they just took the time to figure out how to do it.

No one is holding a gun to your head, forcing you to

work extra hours. However, someone may appear to be making your next raise or promotion contingent on your working overtime. If you feel you're in that position, learn to set some appropriate boundaries (#43). Then waste not a moment finding a worker-friendly company (#68) that values not only your contributions but also your responsibility to yourself and your family.

Working long hours may once have served you, but there's a point of diminishing returns (#54). Few of us can do it forever, and when we do it long term we pay a high price—deterioration of our health, disintegration of our relationships, dissatisfaction with our work, a decrease in what we actually accomplish, and loss of our sense of self.

Decide now that you'll create a work schedule that makes it possible for you to work less and in the process to create a more balanced life. It's your choice. You can pull the plug on forty-hour-plus workweeks any time you choose.

3. Cut Back to Thirty Hours a Week

American workers could take a lesson from the European workplace. In most European countries the thirty-two-hour workweek is mandated by law. In France, it's illegal for *any* employee, from hourly laborers to salaried managers, to work more than thirty-two hours a week. Just think of it: a culture where not even the boss works more than thirty-two hours. And there are currently movements afoot to cut the European workweek even further.

It's easy to assume, because we work more than Europeans do, that the global economic future belongs solely to the United States. But that's not the case. Europe enjoys a possibly unsurpassable global lead in certain important areas of the technological revolution.

For example, European cell phone technology is far more sophisticated and user friendly than ours. Not only have cell phone users in Europe long been able to use their cell phones to check e-mail and to get news bulletins, they can easily place calls to almost anywhere in the world. Because the United States still uses a mishmash of incompatible standards, most U.S. cell phones, depending on the user's carrier and phone, can't be used to place calls across the country and sometimes not even within the state.

Then there's Airbus. In recent years this European consortium captured 55 percent of global-passenger jetliner sales. Competitive pricing, outstanding salesmanship, better safety standards, lower costs, and, again, advanced technology made this coup possible. European innovation and competitiveness also contributed to the development of the smart card, which makes e-commerce easier and more secure, and put Europeans out in front of Americans with this technology, which is vastly superior to ours.

But even if Europe lagged behind the United States in all areas of commerce, so what? Europeans have lives beyond the workplace! And as anyone who's traveled to Western Europe has seen, most Europeans know how to live well and celebrate life, something many Americans have never learned how to do. What is the benefit of so-called global superiority if we're too tired to enjoy it? What is the need for more so-called advancement when we're already so "advanced" we can't see clearly enough to do anything but work harder?

Not only is indiscriminate "progress" wreaking havoc with our lives and our children's lives, but it's also wreaking havoc with our planet. Most debilitating of all, so-called progress is keeping us from maintaining a true connection with each other and with our own souls. It's time for us as a culture to think about progressing less and living more. Let's go back to basics and remember that all we really have to do is put a roof over our heads and meals on the table. Beyond that our time can be better spent enjoying our lives, being with the people we love, creating things we love that don't harm the earth, and contributing something meaningful to the world.

You may not be ready to cut back to a thirty-hour workweek just yet, but I urge you to keep an open mind. Through the process of simplifying you're going to be freeing up lots of time. And once you begin to have the time to enjoy life, and to think and to simply be, you'll see that many things are possible that you may not have been able to consider until now.

Don't rule out the very real possibility of the thirty-two-hour workweek becoming standard in our culture. Anywhere from two-thirds to three-quarters of respondents in numerous recent surveys have said they would gladly take a 20 percent cut in pay for a 20 percent cut in hours. Not many people would have thought thirty years ago that millions of people would institute daily exercise regimens, but we have. Not many people would have thought ten years ago that millions of people would become conscious recyclers, but we have. Not many people would have thought even five years ago that millions of people would be simplifying their lives, but we have. A thirty-two-hour work-week? Yes. It just makes so much sense.

4. Be Sure You Can See the Light
at the End of the Tunnel

Even after you've decided to cut back on the amount of time you work and to create more balance in your life, there may well be times when you want or need to work long hours. You may have to complete an important project, meet a pressing deadline, or establish yourself in a demanding business venture. You may decide to go back to school or to get trained in another field. Or you may need to keep working long hours to hold on to the position you have until you find a job more conducive to a balanced lifestyle.

There are several things you can do to help keep your life from getting out of control during this time.

First, make sure that your decision to step up your work pace is a conscious one. Define your goal for working longer during this period of time. Have a good idea of what that period of time will be. Make sure you understand what other areas of your life will be affected.

Second, rather than going crazy with work, be sure to adopt a pace that honors the rest of your life—your health, your family, your friendships, and your spiritual life. For example, you may not have time each day for your usual hour-long exercise routine, but could you take a brisk fifteen-minute walk? Could you hire someone to take care of the cooking, grocery shopping, laundry, and so forth?

Third, take care of yourself. Make sure you're getting the sleep you need. Take the time to eat properly and have at least one sit-down meal with your family each day. If you have kids, you might want to make the commitment that you'll be there five nights a week to tuck them in, even if it means you go back to work afterward.

Fourth, decide what other commitments—social, community, or extended family—you can let go of. For example, one reader I heard from quit a high-paced life as a journalist in New York and signed a contract to write a book. Shortly thereafter she learned she was pregnant. For the first couple of years she narrowed her daily schedule down so she had only two things to worry about: the baby and the book. She arranged for everything else to be either taken care of by her husband or put on the back burner until she completed her book.

Fifth, let your family and others know well in advance about the decision you've made and the amount of time it entails. Help them think through how they can adjust to your new work schedule.

Sixth, where you reach the light at the end of the tunnel, make the conscious decision to stop. What usually happens when we increase the pace of our work schedule is that before we know it, overwork has become a way of life. When you get to the point where you can cut back, take the time to celebrate with your family and friends. Give yourself credit for making this extra push. Then, after taking a break or time off as a reward, make the conscious decision to resume the normal rhythm of your life. Sit down and figure out what your more relaxed schedule will be and write it into your day planner for the next several months until your new pattern is firmly established.

5. Leave Your Briefcase at the Office

If you regularly work at home after hours, seriously consider what value—if any—that work adds to your life. Also ask yourself what it takes *away* from your life. If you're unable to complete the work you feel you must do during your regular business day, something's out of whack. Perhaps you've let the deluge of mail, phone calls, and other less critical tasks interfere with the work you really should be doing during the day. If that's the case, cut back, rearrange your workload, stop the two-hour business lunches, hire an assistant, delegate more to the staff you already have, or take any one or more of the steps I outline in Part 3.

If you take the time to carefully analyze your after-hours work pattern, you'll see that taking work home is little more than habit. Maybe it was once necessary, but now that you've established the practice, it's hard to stop. Is all the time you spend working at home advancing your career? Is it helping your company? Are you being adequately compensated for it? Are you actually getting that much done? What are you trying to prove? To whom? Are they convinced yet? Will they ever be? Is it adding to your knowledge or wisdom? What secondary benefits are you expecting from this work? What or whom are you avoiding by working at home after hours?

Chances are in a year or two the work you're now doing at home won't matter. Looking back, will you wish you'd spent that time with your kids, with your spouse, exercising to maintain your health, making a contribution to your community or the environment, developing other skills that enhance your feelings of accomplishment, or doing other things you really love to do?

Even if you enjoy your work, overworking throws your life out of kilter. Doing nothing but work drains your energy and closes you off to your inner self. Overworking robs you of the time you need for reflection and for personal, intellectual, and spiritual growth. It keeps you from being open to the inspiration and guidance of your soul. And it keeps you from making the meaningful contribution that comes from a balanced, soul-centered perspective.

If you're ready to cut back the briefcase habit but feel you can't stop completely just yet, start by leaving your briefcase at the office even one or two nights a week. Plan activities that will make it impossible for you to work at home after hours.

6. Stop Working Weekends

If you're going into the office on the weekend, or if you regularly take work home for the weekend, most likely you're not working as effectively during the week as you could be.

Think about what working over the weekend adds to your life. Even if you love your work and are making a momentous contribution to the world, every life requires proportion. Over-work produces stress, and stress produces illness. The National Institutes of Health recently released a study showing that 70 percent of all disease is stress related, and the World Health Organization warns of an increasing incidence of stress-related depression. Fortunately, these are health conditions we can easily do something about.

Start right now. Sit down with your day planner or PDA (personal digital assistant) and block off every single weekend for the next six months. Reserve that time for yourself, for your family, for non—work-related projects, or for simply catching up with the rest of your life. In six months or less you can break the habit of working weekends and, in the process, create a new life for yourself and your family.

Let your boss and coworkers know that as soon as the project you're now engaged in is completed, you won't be taking on any more work that requires you to spend weekends on the job. If you're truly making a difference, and especially if other people are counting on you, the best thing you can do to enhance your value is to take care of yourself.

If your work environment is not conducive to cutting back, this may mean sooner or later you'll be looking for or creating a new job—one that leaves you free on weekends. As we've seen, millions of people are already doing that. And as we'll see in Part 6, more and more companies have come to realize how important it is for their employees to have lives outside the workplace. The nose-to-the-grindstone approach simply doesn't work anymore. In truth, it never did, but we seldom stopped long enough to realize that. It's the creative thought that emerges from balanced lives and from the joy of our leisure time that makes the difference in our ultimate level of creativity and productivity.

7. Eliminate Your Commute

Millions of Americans spend two hours or more each day commuting to and from their place of work. If you're spending this kind of time commuting, you're devoting the equivalent of one month each year just getting to the office. Over a lifetime you're spending roughly three solid years on the road.

For most commuters, time on the road is not only lost time, it's also stress time. Think of the damage you're doing to your spirit—from the noise, traffic, exhaust fumes, inevitable delays, and frayed nerves of fellow commuters. We get used to commuting, and it becomes a way of life. We never stop to think about the absurdity of it.

If you spend an inordinate amount of time getting to and from work, I strongly encourage you to consider alternatives. If you can afford to, make a move that puts you closer to your office, or change jobs so you can work closer to home. Carpool or rearrange your schedule so you can drive to work during off-peak traffic times. Think about the energy you're forfeiting every time you climb on a train or get behind the wheel of the car for a long commute to work. With telecommuting, flex schedules, compressed workweeks, and job sharing, which I discuss in Part 6, you can eliminate or minimize your daily commute. As one reader from upstate New York wrote, "I decided five years ago to take a pay cut and work at home. We live in a modest home and I drive a ten-year-old car. But I don't have to spend an hour and a half commuting into the city, and I get to spend evenings with my kids."

If you must commute for the time being, set a goal to stop commuting within a year or less, so you know the end is in sight. In the meantime, use your commute time to nurture your spirit. If you take the train or bus consciously daydream rather than work (#37). If you drive listen to inspirational or empowering tapes, or sing or hum to beautiful uplifting music. Or learn to enjoy the silence. Remember that when there is silence, there is room for thought.

Whatever you do, don't spend your commute time working—that's the same thing as taking work home from the office. It robs you of time in which to simply be.

8. Take Your Vacation

Time magazine recently ran the following report:

> If you're a working man, don't pass up your family vacation. Time off is rejuvenating, according to research presented to the American Psychosomatic Society. A study of 12,338 men ages 35 to 57 found that, with other factors controlled, men who took annual vacations were 21% less likely to die during the 16 year study period than non-vacationers—and 32% less likely to die of coronary heart disease. The findings add to evidence showing that cutting stress is good for you.

What is fascinating about this blurb is that *Time* considered it newsworthy. Don't we already know that time off is rejuvenating? Don't we already know that reducing stress is good for us? Do we have to be cajoled into taking our vacations because there's a high incidence of coronary heart disease in those who don't do so? But if the truth were known, many American workers are not taking vacations. The United States is the most vacation-starved country in the industrialized world.

Once again, Europe takes the lead. In total hours, we work two months longer each year than Europeans do. European workers, after only one year on the job, get five full weeks of paid vacation, and this increases to a full six weeks after the second year. And every worker takes it. It's time for us to wise up. Not only should we be taking our vacations, we should be lobbying our employers and our elected representatives for at least a full month or more of vacation time each year.

Will you remember a year from now, three years from now, five years from now what the "crisis" was that kept you from taking your vacation or that kept you from enjoying it? Not a chance. But there's a chance you'll remember a wonderful vacation. Take every single vacation day that's coming to you. Even if your time away from the office isn't memorable, just being away from the pressures of work will do your body and your soul and your psyche good.

Arrange your schedule so you never have to call your office when you're on vacation. One of the reasons we come back from vacations more exhausted than when we left is that we spend our time worrying about work. We fall into the trap of thinking that things can't go on without us. Or maybe we're afraid they will move on and we'll be left behind. Let go of those ideas and take your full vacation time. Stop worrying about what's happening back at the office. If you're seizing your time well, as I'll discuss in Part 2, and delegating properly, things will be taken care of in your absence. If they aren't, it's not the end of the world. What's the worst that could happen if you're not in touch with your office for a week or two? Make the best arrangements you can, then relax and enjoy your time off. You've earned it.

At the very least promise yourself you'll never again brag about not taking your vacation.

9. Take a Sabbatical

How would you like to take a six-month sabbatical? How about a year's sabbatical? Think you couldn't possibly take that much time off? Think your boss would never go for the idea? Think you can't afford it? Think again. According to Hope Dlugozima, James Scott, and David Sharp in their book *Six Months Off* (Holt, 1996), more than two out of ten American companies offer some kind of sabbatical program, and more than seven in ten offer personal leaves of absence, which people often use for the same purpose.

What's even better is that fully one-third of American companies will soon be offering sabbaticals. Already many companies, including IBM, Apple Computer, Intel, Time Inc., Xerox, American Express, McDonald's, and numerous others offer sabbaticals, a benefit employees covet. Many smaller businesses are also getting on the bandwagon. Why? Companies are starting to *get* it. They've learned that it enhances the bottom line when they give valued employees a chance to recharge their batteries. Most employers find that people return refreshed and ready to start working again with new enthusiasm.

Also, companies have found it's easier and less expensive in the long run to provide extended breaks than to replace employees who have burned out due to long hours. Companies are also realizing that employees value the chance to work on their own terms. In fact, employees are demanding it. Companies that don't understand this are losing out on the best talent.

In addition to allowing the time off for sabbaticals, many companies are also footing the bill, in full or in part. And where company resources are not provided, there are many grants, scholarships, fellowships, and exchange programs available that make it possible for practically anyone—from top executives to relative newcomers to the world of work—to get the break they need from their work lives. Check out *Six Months Off* for a complete listing of such programs.

While on sabbatical you'll have the opportunity to energize your present career or start a new one, revitalize an old hobby or create a different one, go back to school to learn other skills or explore a field you've always been fascinated by but never had the time to pursue. A sabbatical will make it possible for you to regain your health or your sanity, to travel and experience new cultures, and to reconnect with your spouse and your kids. Perhaps most important, taking a break from your current work schedule will give you the opportunity to step back and discover your life's true purpose and to make certain your work life is a meaningful expression of that purpose.

10. Take Time to Think

Calculate the amount of time you'd gain by implementing the ideas outlined so far. Having time is absolutely essential. You need time to *think*. You need time to *be* with your thoughts, to mull them over, to change them again until you light upon the right thoughts that will guide you where you want to go. You need time to figure out where you are—with a project you're in the middle of, with the direction your career is headed, with the course your life is taking. It's because we haven't had time to think that we've allowed our work lives to get so out of control.

It's challenging to turn one's attention away from the foam of events and to perceive the most important currents. But it's absolutely vital for our survival and, ultimately, for the survival of the planet that we learn to do so. It's through having time that you can create the balance you need to be happy and productive. It's through having time that you can become engulfed in the mystery and grandeur of life. It's through having time that you discover something supremely indefinable about the meaning of your own life that only you can discern. In our culture we don't trust thought sufficiently. But where else can we find the power to change our destiny? Only in thought. When you create time in which to think, you'll acquire those subtle perceptions that will transform your life.

With technology and the business world changing so fast, there's never been a greater need to have the time to determine the right direction for you to take. Since you can't know or do it all, it's vital that you learn to take the time to sense what you need to know and do. We simply can't afford—either as individuals or as a species—to allow the pace of our lives to keep us from consciously determining where our technological and creative processes are taking us.

11. Decide to Do It

The son and daughter of a friend of mine are in their early thirties; both are employed in the computer industry. They've been working around the clock for ten years, most recently for a company they hope will soon go public and make each of them millionaires. They're constantly on call. Neither of them has a life away from their cell phones. They can't make long-term plans. Neither of them has had a true vacation in years. Just getting several days off recently to go to a family wedding was a monumental task. They're exhausted; they want to stop, but they don't know how.

When you're in the middle of such a hectic work life, it feels as if there is some earthshaking thing you have to do in order to stop. But starting to stop is truly quite easy. All you have to do is *decide* to do it. It's as simple as that. All you have to do is wake up. All you have to do is decide that you've had enough. That's it. Once you make that decision, the stopping will start.

Part of what makes cutting back seem so hard is that it requires a more conscious decision than the process we went through to build up to our present work schedules.

Think back to how you began. Most likely you established your present work mode without thinking too much about it. You started with a nominal forty-hour-a-week job with the understanding that you'd be willing to put in whatever time it took to get the job done. Little by little you were staying later and later at the office, or maybe you were going into the office on weekends, "just to get caught up." You might very naturally have been trying to impress your boss or your coworkers with your commitment and dedication to the work you were taking on and with your ability to do the job. Perhaps you jumped into a position that was beyond you and felt you had to put in extra time just to learn the ropes. Who among us hasn't done that? It's possible you were moving up the ladder, and with each move you had to continue to prove to yourself or to others that you were up to the job. With each advancement it was less likely you'd be going back to a forty-hour week. It may not even have occurred to you to do so.

At the time, working long hours didn't seem out of the ordinary. You were no doubt surrounded by others who were doing the same thing. Without consciously thinking about what you were doing—other than trying to live up to your goal to succeed—you were all moving "forward" together. One step up the ladder led to another, and before you knew what had happened you were working far beyond forty hours a week. Now, thanks to the latest cell phone, fax, and pager technology, you're plugged in 24/7. Chances are you didn't *decide* you'd work an outrageous number of hours a week. You just sort of fell into the routine.

But we seldom just fall into cutting back. For most of us it has to be a conscious decision. The momentum has been going in the other direction for so long that it feels unnatural to slow down. You have to be committed to doing so. This isn't to say that you can't take cutting back one step at a time. Most certainly you can. You can start by taking any one of the steps in this part. A journey of a thousand miles begins with the first step. Each step you take will make it easier to take another one. You just decide to do it. Then begin.

TWO

Learning to Seize Time

12. Get a Jump on Tomorrow

One of the primary objectives in simplifying our lives at work is to free up time so we can create balance between our work and all the other areas of our lives. If there's one thing I've learned, it's that time is seldom handed out; we have to seize it for ourselves. Throughout this part we'll be looking at ways to find more time so you can work less.

One easy way to seize time is to get into the habit of taking five minutes at the end of your day to clean up your space and get organized for the next day's work. Even if you're in the middle of a project you want to continue with the next day, you'll find it helpful to straighten up your papers and files and put away books, folders, notes, and other materials for which you won't have an immediate need.

Then take a couple of minutes to figure out what tasks you want to start in on in the morning. Prioritize these and put them on a note to yourself, which you can leave in the center of your cleared desk so you can't miss it when you sit down to work again.

The benefits of taking this simple step are fourfold. First, it gives you an opportunity to take stock of what you achieved during the day and give yourself credit for the things you accomplished. There will always be tasks that don't get done, but when you rejoice in what you did do, it sets your mental and psychic stage for doing even better tomorrow and gives you a sense of completion and satisfaction with your work.

Second, it sends a signal to your psyche that you're now wrapping up your work for the day. ("Okay, I've given my time and energy to my work. Now it's time to devote my energies to something else.") Without this conscious break, your mind can easily continue to be occupied by niggling worries and concerns that keep you from enjoying your evening and, in the extreme, keep you from having a good night's sleep.

Third, when you know exactly what to start with in the morning, it's so much easier to jump right in and do it. You won't have to waste those valuable first minutes of your prime work time—which can easily stretch to half an hour or more—trying to figure out where to begin.

Fourth, when you purposefully wrap up for the day and get ready for tomorrow, you put your subconscious mind to work helping you organize your thinking and your approach to the next day. You can then begin your evening activities without having to be consciously involved in the process. You'll find you'll be able to come to your work in the morning with a clear head and fresh insights.

13. Learn to Schedule Carefully

Whenever you make an appointment, figure out how long it will take, set a realistic schedule so you can be there on time, then don't allow anything to distract you from it. For example, if you need to leave at two forty-five to get to your three o'clock appointment, don't take or make a quick phone call at two forty. There's no such thing as a quick phone call when you're in a hurry. If you end up with five extra minutes on your hands, train yourself to sit quietly and enjoy it. Or use that time to think about how you can make the best use of the meeting. Or leave five minutes earlier and walk or drive to the appointment at a more leisurely pace.

When scheduling meetings or appointments, accurately calculate drive times and other factors, such as heavy traffic, road repairs, and weather that could cause you to be late. Most time management systems are broken down into thirty-minute and even fifteen-minute increments. When I have a three o'clock appointment that I know will take me thirty minutes to reach, I write "leave" in the two-thirty slot so I'll remember to leave on time. Having to rush is such an insidious time-robber—when you're worried about not being able to get there on time, you can't savor the ride. When you arrive late, your energy is scattered and you feel out of sorts; not a productive beginning. Make the effort to create a tempo that allows you to enjoy whatever it is you do.

Learn to be selective when scheduling tasks, projects, and appointments. Get into the habit of asking yourself "Do I really need to do this now?" or "Do I need to do it at all?" Look over your schedule for the past month or so and ask yourself what you could have eliminated. Much of what we spend our time doing doesn't need to be done. Making wise choices is one of the most effective ways to seize time. Also, be cautious about double scheduling. Think about how often you've promised to be in two places at the same time.

As much as possible, avoid long boring office meetings that drain your time and energy. Brainstorm with your staff and co-workers to develop creative ways to make your meetings more productive. Use an agenda, establish a realistic time frame for each item on the agenda, and stick to the time allotted for each topic.

Avoid scheduling early appointments that will disrupt your morning routine.

Say no to *every* new request for your time for the next month. When you say no to everything, it minimizes the guilt. "Sorry, I'm not taking on any new projects for a month or two." Saying no to all requests also makes it easier because you don't have to take the time to decide.

Minimize the number of lunch dates and other work-related gatherings you engage in each week.

Give yourself a break. How long has it been since you took a morning or afternoon break? Breaks used to be standard practice in the workplace. Recent research has shown that most workers feel too overwhelmed to take even a few minutes off every couple of hours to restore their energy. It's important for your health and well-being to do so. Write those times into your daily schedule and honor them. In Part 3 you'll find ways to take breaks that'll make you more productive and thereby free up even more time.

14. Put an Extra Day into Your Vacation Schedule

Have you ever wished you could take an extra vacation day just to recover from your vacation? Do you dread coming back from a vacation or business trip because you know you'll have to face two weeks' worth of mail, messages, and other work? Have you ever thought of sneaking into the office before everyone knows you're back so you can take care of the work that's been piling up before you get overwhelmed by the new problems you know you'll immediately be swamped with?

Here's a simple solution. Next time you take your vacation, give yourself an extra day to get caught up. Let's say you're due back in the office on the 15th. Let your clients, associates, and coworkers know you'll be back in the office for business on the 16th or even on the 17th. This way, when you return to the office on the 15th you have a day or two to catch up. A day or two won't make any difference at all to your associates, but it'll make a big difference to you.

Set up an automatic reply to any e-mail messages that arrive in your absence, giving your "back in the office for business" date.

Leave a similar message on your voice mail, or instruct your staff to convey the same message to anyone asking about your return. If you're discreet, and train your staff and coworkers to be discreet as well, you can get fully caught up before anyone even knows you're back.

If someone tries to engage you in conversation or attempts to dragoon you into a new work activity, don't hesitate to set a firm boundary: "I'm not officially back until the 17th. I'll call you then." Then get back to catching up on the old stuff.

15. Double Your Estimate

Before you agree to take on a time-consuming project, force yourself to think carefully about the amount of time it actually will take, then double your estimate. *Things always take twice as long to complete as you think they will.* Failing to accurately determine how long a particular task will take puts you under tremendous pressure. Your other work suffers in the process, which creates even more stress, which in turn robs you of time and lessens your efficiency. You end up in another vicious cycle of working, often overtime, to meet one unrealistic deadline, while falling behind with everything else.

Use this process, which you can adapt to your circumstances, before you agree to any deadline:

- Begin by asking for at least twenty-four hours. "I'll let you know first thing tomorrow morning when I can have this project finished." Or use some variation of "Let me think about this and I'll get back to you."

- Then arrange for a few minutes of uninterrupted time. Close the door, put up a "Do Not Disturb" sign, turn off the phone, whatever. Then carefully calculate the amount of time you'll need to complete the work.

- Make a list of all the tasks that comprise this job: research, doing the outline, making phone calls, collecting data, thinking through the data, writing up the rough draft, getting associates to critique it, doing the final write-up, and so on.

- Indicate the amount of time you think it will take to complete each task.

- Take into account the other work you'll have to complete, as well.

- Tally up the time.

- Then double the time you've estimated.

- If you're contemplating a new project, something you've never done before, and you're uncertain about what will be required to complete it and how long it will take, put your list of tasks on your night table before you go to sleep. Then take five minutes in the morning before you get out of bed, while you're still in that semiconscious but receptive state, to look over your list. Be sure it includes everything you'll need to do to produce the outstanding results you want for this job. You can get valuable information from your subconscious mind early in the morning, before your conscious mind takes over for the day.

- Then enthusiastically commit to a realistic completion date.

If necessary, be ready to support your decision with details from your list. "Jack tells me it'll take at least two weeks for him to get the data from R&D."

Don't forget that work expands to fill the time allotted for it. The goal here, using both your conscious and your subconscious mind, is to get good at making accurate estimates. You want to allow enough time to get the job done without stress while at the same time making sure you don't waste time by overestimating how long it will take.

16. Use Phone Technology
to Your Advantage

Modern technology holds the potential to save us huge amounts of time, but often it consumes our time instead. Technology seduces us with promises of ease and freedom, but we can quickly get so caught up in it that we end up being trapped by it.

The telephone is a perfect example of a technology that can distract us from our work. Telephones, and all their accessories and ancillary parts, including cell phones, pagers, beepers, call waiting, call forwarding, caller ID, and the like, offer incredible benefits. But many people are starting to realize that phones, especially cell phones and beepers, whose numbers we often give out unthinkingly, keep us tethered around the clock. Not only does this rob us of precious time, but it's an invitation to abuse. When people can reach you 24/7, they will.

Here are some simple and painless steps you can take to make sure your phones work for you rather than against you:

- Be discriminating in giving out your cell phone number. Just because other people choose to be available around the clock, it doesn't mean you have to. Use your cell phone to get help if you need it or to communicate with coworkers and family members when there's a change of plans. But be sure to ask others not to overuse it. And don't hesitate to turn it off when you don't want to be interrupted.

- All self-respecting businesses have business hours. Let callers know what your work hours are, then be firm. When you give out your cell phone or your home number, set limits on when you'll be available:

    "If you must call me at home, I'm available between 8 and 10 P.M. Monday through Thursday."

    "Please don't call me after 10 P.M."

    "Please don't call me on weekends unless it's urgent."

    Most people will respect your requests; if you find that certain people do not, don't hesitate to set them straight. If you find it challenging to establish these boundaries, see Part 4 for ways to make that easier. And if your employer isn't receptive to your requests, maybe it's time to find a worker-friendly office, where everyone recognizes the basic need we all have for balance in our lives.

- Rather than allowing the phone to interrupt your work constantly, set aside a specific time to make and return calls. Let people know what that time is. For example, my best writing time is between 9 A.M. and 3 P.M. During that time I turn off the ringer on my phone and let voice mail take messages. People who call me regularly don't expect a return call until midafternoon. I do my phone work then, and eliminate phone interruptions during my prime work time. Make a similar arrangement for your schedule.

- Monitor your phone use carefully. If necessary, for the next few weeks, keep track of the amount of time you spend on the phone. You may find much of that time is wasted. If you're staying late to finish work you didn't get completed, or taking work home from the office because you were idling away time on the phone, here's a perfect area in which you can seize time.

- Turn your phones off after hours or when you don't want to be interrupted. Break the habit of answering the phone whenever it rings. One way to get over that sense of urgency is to arrange with a like-minded coworker, a friend, or a family member to call you intermittently for a week or more, so you can see how you jump-to when a call comes in. You can return the favor; we all need help overcoming this automatic response. Or simply keep track of your incoming calls for a day or two and become aware of how you respond. Once you see your Pavlovian reaction to a ringing phone—and see how often a ringing phone robs you of your precious time—it'll be easier to break the pattern.

- If you need to work with the phone off in order to have a stretch of uninterrupted time but are concerned about missing calls, use the company voice mail service or sign up for voice mail with your phone service provider if you work at home. This is an efficient and inexpensive way to make certain you don't miss calls. Just be sure to discipline yourself so you avoid the habit of checking for messages every five minutes.

- If you need to work with the phone off but have kids or an ailing parent you want to be available to, get a pager or have a second line installed just for them, and make sure no one else gets that number.
- Use voice mail or answering machines to convey information rather than force others to play phone tag.
- Turn off your pager, beeper, and cell phone in restaurants, theaters, and supermarkets, and on the street and public transportation, such as buses, trains, and airplanes. These situations used to be free time, time when we could escape from the constant interruptions of the outside world, when we could think or simply enjoy the moment. Now, not only are phones in those situations an annoyance to the people who're forced to listen to a conversation they're not interested in, robbing them of their own escape, but indiscriminate phone use eats up your time without your even being aware of it.

17. Be Selective in Giving Out
Your E-mail Address

I recently sat next to a woman in an airport who moaned out loud when she checked her e-mail and found she had over two hundred messages. Like most of us, e-mail is a relatively new factor in her work life but now a significant one. She regularly gets several hundred messages a day, many of which she said are unnecessary. She now spends two to three hours each day dealing with and responding to e-mail.

Electronic mail can be a tremendous simplifier when used consciously and efficiently, but when we let it get out of hand, it quickly adds several more levels of complexity to our lives. It robs us of valuable time without our being aware of it. If you find you're overwhelmed by e-mail, here are some things to consider:

- As with your cell phone, be selective about giving out your e-mail address. And when you do, ask people not to send you information you don't absolutely need to see.

- Think twice before adding your e-mail address to your business card. (In fact, think twice about whether you really need a business card. Resist the temptation to play the let's-exchange-business-cards game unless it truly supports your work.)

- Ask people to delete your name from "automatic-send" e-mail lists, especially those who send you jokes you have no interest in reading.

- Ask your employees, employer, and coworkers to be more efficient in using e-mail.

- Let your boss know if the volume of e-mail is preventing you from doing an efficient job. Many companies recognize that e-mail has gotten out of hand and have set up policies for using e-mail, as well as voice mail, to its best advantage.

- When you receive e-mail that is longer than it needs to be, politely ask the sender to be more brief. This will save both of you time.

- Turn off the beep on your e-mail system that announces that you have mail, and check and retrieve your messages only once a day— less if possible. If necessary, let your contacts know when you check your mail and how quickly they might expect a response. Just because the in-flow of e-mail is constant and instantaneous doesn't mean you have to respond constantly and instantaneously. Don't allow other people's hurry sickness to run your life. I use e-mail for my nationally syndicated newspaper column, and check it once a week in the time slot I've set aside. I've let readers know that relevant letters will be addressed in future columns, so there is no expectation for an immediate response.

- Learn what e-mail options are available to you for filtering the e-mail programs you use. Most e-mail programs allow you to automatically transfer to the trash any messages you don't want.

- Be firm with yourself. Before you press send, think about whether this message really needs to go out. Consider what unnecessary work it might create for you and the person you're sending it to.

- Don't respond to junk e-mail.

- Don't get personal in your office e-mail. With cyberveillance, companies are now able to monitor employees' computer activity—every message sent, every Web site visited, every key stroked. Even "deleted" information can be retrieved for your boss to read. Realize that legally your employer has the right to read and monitor your e-mail, and compose your communications accordingly.

18. Eliminate the Junk

It's estimated that the typical executive receives over two hundred pieces of unsolicited mail each month. Over half of this can easily be stopped. Simply send a postcard to the Mail Preference Service, P.O. Box 9008, Farmingdale, NY 11735. Ask them to remove your name from junk mail lists. Be vigorous in eliminating the mail you don't want. It robs you of time and energy you need for more important things.

If credit card offers flood your office (or your home), call the Equifax, Trans Union, Novas, and Experian credit bureaus at 888-5-OPT OUT, and request they not use your name.

The junk mail you receive can be minimized or eliminated entirely: Every time you order by phone or mail or make charitable contributions, ask that your name not be sold or passed on to other organizations. Also, check out www.metrokc.gov/nwpc; click on "Reduce Business Junk Mail." This service is sponsored by the Seattle-based National Waste Prevention Coalition.

The Web site includes information on how to have your business removed from lists and explains how companies and organizations have reduced unwanted mail.

Be diligent about calling the 800 numbers on mailers you no longer wish to receive. Ask them to remove your name.

Don't allow personal mail, junk or otherwise, to be sent to your office, or office-related mail, junk or otherwise, to arrive at your home. Keeping the two separate will help you avoid dealing with office-related matters at home and vice versa. It'll also eliminate carrying stacks of mail back and forth between home and office, material that can easily get lost, causing you to lose even more precious time.

The average American now spends the equivalent of five days a year opening and reading junk mail; over a forty-year career, that's nearly a year out of your life. You'll be amazed at how much time you can save by carefully monitoring who gets your name, address, and phone numbers.

19. Minimize the Paper Glut

Mel Goodes, the CEO who grew Warner-Lambert from $9 billion to nearly $60 billion in seven years, says that when he first came to the job he got rid of two-thirds of the paper that came across his desk.

Become aware of the endless stream of paper that flows into your life on a daily basis that keeps you from concentrating on what's truly important. We spend untold hours taking it in, glancing at it, sorting through it, reading it, stacking it on a corner of the desk, glancing through it again, setting it aside, then later trying to find it again, not knowing what to do with it, finally deciding what to do with it, filing it, passing it on to clutter up someone else's space, setting it aside to clutter up our own space, or tossing it out.

If you don't have a method for handling it, paper can be overwhelming. My favorite system of handling it only once is described below (#22). But the secret to simplifying in this area is, as much as possible, to stop the flow at its source.

Make a point over the next month of analyzing the paper, magazines, newsletters, mail, reports, memos, notices, and junk you have to handle regularly, keeping track of the amount of time you spend dealing with it all. Then take a cold, hard look at what you can eliminate. Here are some things to consider:

- Take your name off the office routing lists of reports and memos except for those you absolutely must see.

- Cancel subscriptions to the newsletters, magazines, and business reports that duplicate each other or that you never have time to read. If you can't find the time for it, it's not that important to you. Or read only every other issue. So much of what appears in these sources is repetitive, or includes things you already know, don't need to know, or don't want to know. Keep one or two sources you find truly helpful, then let the rest go.

- Whenever possible, sign up for electronic newsletters, magazines, and newspapers for the information you must have.

- To minimize the amount of paper overall, share magazines and newsletters with your staff and coworkers via a routing list. This works well when each person abides by the rules and passes the publication on to the next person on the list within a specified period of time. Make sure everyone understands how much time he or she has before it has to be passed on. If necessary, have one person be responsible for keeping a hard copy, say for six months, in a central file. That keeps the material out of your space yet accessible.

- Train an assistant to read magazines for you, highlighting information you need to see.

- Use computer faxes rather than paper faxes.

- Avoid printing e-mail. Save it to a computer file if it's important, and back it up on a zip disk in a workable filing system. Delete it if it isn't important. (At this point, a CD-ROM burner is a good way to go for *permanent* storage of information.)

- Schedule a time—maybe the first of each month—for deleting piled-up e-mail you haven't answered and never will.

- Don't hold on to e-mails just to save the address. Transfer the address to your electronic address book and delete the original.

- Get into the habit of downloading critical information from the Net into a computer file rather than printing or asking that hard copies to be mailed to you.

- Keep in mind that close to 90 percent of the paper you keep in files is never used or looked at again. Having all that paper on hand makes the task of finding what you need when you need it more difficult, and requires additional time and effort. And how often do you ever actually need it? Not enough to justify keeping it.

It's now possible to retrieve from the Internet practically any information you might need, usually far more easily than finding it in your paper files. We're often still living as if copy machines, zip disks, Palm Pilots, printers, and the Internet don't exist. It's time to move consciously and intelligently into the information age. We've got magnificent technology to simplify our work habits, but often we're still holding on to the old methods as well. Living in both worlds complicates our lives.

20. Learn to Grasp Information Quickly

Even after you've reduced the flow of paper, you'll still be inundated with data. After all, most of us are exposed to more new information in a day than previous generations were exposed to in a lifetime. It's so easy to get overwhelmed by all the information and to feel helpless about it. This factor alone is responsible for the high levels of stress many people experience today.

Keep in mind that, thanks to movies, television, and computer usage—as well as the tremendous amounts of information we're exposed to every day in books, magazines, newspapers, fliers, billboards, and even junk mail—we've been building into our systems the capacity to work very quickly through a vast body of information. Think about that for a moment. Internalize it. See and acknowledge yourself as someone who has that capacity, and move into that new way of being. Use this newly ingrained capacity to become a wise consumer of information.

The people who are successful now and those who will be

successful in the future are those who understand intuitively or have made it their business to learn how to grasp information quickly. One way they do that is to make sure they're not needlessly giving up their time to someone else's idea of what they need to know.

Take advantage of local adult education programs or any courses or seminars your employer offers that will help you with your thinking and decision-making skills.

Check out *The 100% Brain Course*, available through Creative Alternatives, 463 Kern Springs Road, Woodstock, VA 22664; (863) 675-6859, and braincourse.com. This training manual provides over two hundred mental exercises to improve your memory and expand your learning capacity.

Learn to sing. We now know, thanks to *The Mozart Effect* by Don Campbell (Avon Books, 1997), that students who sing or play an instrument score up to fifty-one points higher on the SATs than the national average. Music can strengthen your mind, unlock your creativity, and even heal your body. Learning to sing can not only help you expand your intelligence but also help you find your voice so you can become a powerful presence in the world. Check out voicesunlimitedonline.com for information on voice enhancement tapes and personal and corporate seminars that can not only boost your learning capabilities but also enhance your communication skills.

At the same time you're expanding your grasp of information, you must learn to be adaptable. People now change careers half a dozen times over the course of their lives. Train yourself to keep looking ahead to see how your skills can be enhanced or changed to meet the changing workplace.

Realize that even with your increased ability to assimilate massive amounts of information, you'll never know it all. And you don't need to. You know what you know, and, as long as you're open to continuing to learn, if there's something else you need to know, you'll adapt and learn it. Much of what you learn today will be outdated information by tomorrow anyway, so don't get too excited about it.

Albert Einstein believed that imagination is much more important than information. Let go of the perceived need to know it all, and take some of the time you're seizing to sit quietly and daydream, or go play and have some fun.

21. Get Organized

Once you've cut back on the amount of stuff that comes across your desk you'll have a lot less stuff to organize, but you'll still need to be organized. Without an organizational system, you'll spend far too much time spinning your wheels looking for things and being frustrated, which only adds to the time drain.

There are tons of books on how to get organized for today's business world, including information on how to set up paper filing systems, e-mail, faxes, computer files, and Internet information. If organization is a weak point for you, I urge you to find a system you can adapt to your particular needs.

People always ask me how I stay organized. In terms of the big picture, here are some things that work for me.

First, I follow the cardinal rule of organization: I have a place for everything and keep everything in its place except when I'm using it. When I'm finished using it, I put it back. This is a habit that's easy to develop if you put your mind to it. Once this becomes a habit, everything else you need to do to be organized is so much easier.

Second, I keep my desk clear of everything except a vase of fresh flowers and the materials that relate to the project I'm currently working on. And I always take five minutes at the end of my work time to neaten it up for the next morning. Anything related to any other project is kept in a folder in a file drawer immediately at hand, but not on the desk.

To make this workable, I batch my work as much as possible. For example, I write in the morning, with the papers I need spread over my desk. When my writing time is over for the day, I straighten everything up (put away related files, close up reference materials and put them on the nearby shelf, stack the papers I'm working on, etc.).

Then I pick up my messages and handle phone calls, deal with faxes or e-mail, or work on an editing project. Any notes or material I need for these tasks are kept in a folder in my file drawer immediately at hand. This way papers related to phone calls don't get comingled with papers related to my writing project or get misplaced. When I'm finished with them, they go right back into the folder and into the file drawer.

Your work may not lend itself to such simple categories, but perhaps you could adapt a similar system. For example, if you need to answer the phone throughout the day as well as handle paper flow, you might keep the phone on a sideboard or on top of a two-drawer file cabinet next to your desk. That space would be for phone work, messages, and related papers and tasks, while your desk could be kept clear for the paper flow or computer work. The trick is to set up your file drawer so it can hold, within immediate reach, folders with all the materials and paper you're not currently working on.

Third, except for my computer, I keep only one writing tool at hand. For years I had a cup filled with pens and pencils on my desk. Invariably I'd end up with pencils all over the place, but I could never put my hand on one when I needed it. For the past ten years I've used the same mechanical pencil with a refillable eraser for most of my handwritten work, such as editing, making notes, or entering phone messages in my day planning system. I use only this one pencil, and I always know where it is—it's either on my desk or at my planner, which is next to the phone. (It's sometimes hard to let go of those old Type A personality traits!) I got rid of the cup of writing implements, and I keep lead and erasers for refills, and a backup pencil should I ever need one, in a nearby supply drawer.

Fourth, I keep a neat stack of scrap writing paper next to

the phone for quick notes, which I immediately file or, by the end of the day, transfer to the appropriate computer document or filed document as needed, then discard into the recycling bin. If you use a Palm Pilot–type device, you can eliminate the scrap paper and most of the Post-it Notes.

22. Handle It Once

When you've minimized the paper glut by eliminating the junk mail and cutting back on the magazines and newsletters you don't need to see, the daily challenge of dealing with the incoming mail is so much simpler. The next step is to set up a system of handling your mail so it goes through your hands a minimum number of times, preferably once.

For most of your day-to-day mail, this is an easy goal to achieve. Here's my approach, which can be adapted to your workload, schedule, and circumstances. (This system can also be adapted to your e-mail and home mail.)

Deal with your mail at the same time every day. If necessary, mark off the time on your schedule in the same way you would an appointment with a client or colleague, and let nothing interfere with that time. Avoid the temptation to flip through your mail at a time other than your regularly scheduled time. Develop the discipline to just let it sit there in your mailbox until your mail-handling time; alas, it won't go anywhere. As you whittle the mail down to a manageable flow, cut back the time you set aside to handle it. But for starters, schedule at least an hour—more if you know you'll need it.

At your mail time, pick up the stack of mail from your mailbox. When appropriate, call the junk mailers to remove your name from their lists. Then toss all the junk mail in the recycling bin.

Sort the mail into three categories:

1. Handle or Read Now.

2. Handle Later (when you have the necessary information).

3. Read Later (when you have the time).

Your goal should be to soon reach a point where you have only one category: Handle or Read Now. If you faithfully schedule the time to deal with the mail each day, you can easily get to the point where you can handle all of it in a brief period of time at one sitting.

Take the stack of Handle Now mail, prioritize it, and respond to it, delegate it, or deal with it, as necessary. If you type the response to your correspondence on a computer, think hard before making a hard copy. Keep a copy in your appropriate computer file, and always back up your files. Remember, much of what we keep in paper files is never looked at again. Whenever possible, respond by e-mail, or write a response note directly on the incoming letter and return it to the sender.

Next, take the stack of mail to be answered or dealt with later and put it in an easily accessible folder labeled Handle Later, which you keep in a file drawer near you, but not on your desk.

As you put each letter or note into the Handle Later folder, make a corresponding to-do note in your time management system, on a date when you will have the information you need in order to respond. Also note where the originating document is (e.g., "Sales Figures. Handle Later file"). When that date comes, you'll have the letter in your Handle Later file and can deal with it during your mail-handling time. If the day you've marked on your schedule arrives and you still don't have the information, put a note regarding this task on the future date when you expect to have it.

Now take the Read Now stack, prioritize it, and read through what you have time for. If you don't have time to finish it all, then put it in the Read Later file and deal with it the next day during your mail-handling time slot.

If you regularly don't have time to finish your Read Now material at your daily mail-handling time, then either schedule more time each day or schedule a block of time each week or even several times a week to do the reading you need to do. I set aside several hours one afternoon a week for reading and, if necessary, to finish any correspondence I didn't have time to do in my daily mail-handling time slot.

If you're routinely unable to finish the reading in the time you've allotted, either schedule more time or look realistically at ways to cut back on the material you think you have to read.

When you return from vacation or a business trip and face a mile-high stack of mail, take a similar approach, but schedule more time each day for a week or two until you catch up. Next trip, write the extra time in on your schedule *before* you leave for vacation. Or put an extra vacation day into your schedule (#14). If possible, arrange ahead of time for your mail—or the bulk of it—to be handled by someone else in your absence.

If you're able to deal with today's mail in less than the time you've allotted, pull out your Read Later file and read what you didn't have time for the day before.

If it takes less time than you've scheduled to handle the day's mail, and you've taken care of everything in your Later files, reward yourself: Leave early and enjoy your free time.

23. Learn Basic Computer Troubleshooting Skills

If you're not yet computer literate, and your success on the job or your livelihood depends on your computer functioning well when you need it, don't wait to be asked. Take a course or a series of courses. Or have a friend, one of your kids, or a consultant teach you what you have to know so you can avoid not only the lost time, but the stress caused by computer downtime.

This doesn't mean you have to become a computer techie. But learn the basic steps you need to know to get out of a computer crash so that, when possible, you can save time by correcting the problem yourself. If you're unable to get the system up and running on your own, knowing the basics will save you time with the company troubleshooter or with your own consultant because you'll be able to give a detailed and informed report about how the problem occurred. Or, with some basic knowledge, you may be able to implement the recommendations made by a technical consultant over the phone and thereby save the time and money you lose when equipment has to be sent back to the factory. Without some technical experience or training, you're likely to have far more downtime.

Children learn computers quickly because they aren't afraid and they can easily get lost in the joy of the learning process. They keep experimenting and learning, even when the computer gives them one problem after another. Keep your mind open to the learning process. Ask questions whenever possible. When the most cost- and time-effective strategy is to hire a trained consultant to handle your technical problems, do so, but don't succumb to feelings of helplessness. Keep learning whatever you can about the equipment you use. Little by little you'll find you're able to solve technical problems that once seemed insurmountable.

It's so easy to fall into the trap of feeling that you're the only one who's overwhelmed by computer technology. But millions of us feel overwhelmed. Because things are changing so fast— and systems often get more and more complicated under the guise of getting simpler—even experienced technical consultants frequently feel overwhelmed.

Invest $50 in a manual—or have your company buy one for you—that will get you through the most common snafus you're likely to encounter with your computer. Then take the time to study it just enough so you have a reasonable idea where in the manual you can quickly find the help you need when a problem occurs.

Be sure you learn how to organize your computer files efficiently.

Here are some basics you can learn that will help you move quickly and efficiently through many of the computer problems you are likely to encounter:

How to restart your computer when it crashes

How and when to run disk maintenance software such as Symantic's Norton Disk Doctor, available for both Macs and PCs (Run it after every crash, at the very least.)

How and when to reinstall your peripheral software

How to get the maximum benefit from your software, including your e-mail software

How to configure and backup your computer for e-mail and Net access so you can easily reconfigure them when you lose the configurations after a crash. Keep a hard copy of your configurations for easy access.

How to download software updates from the Internet

If you're connected to the Internet, be sure you have antivirus software and know how to install and use it. Talk to your consultant to see if you need to purchase firewall software for additional protection for your circumstances. This software can be expensive, but if your situation warrants it, it can be worth the cost.

You probably already know to never, ever buy or acquire the first version of any new computer hardware or software. Unless you enjoy endless frustration, wait for the later versions, in which most problems have been fixed because of the complaints registered by people who didn't know enough to wait. Then you can avoid the time-consuming task of having to make your new system compatible with the old one by trial and error.

Get into the habit of keeping detailed notes when you begin having problems with your system. Note exactly what you were doing just before a problem started and exactly how the computer responded with each step you took. This history can often save your consultant a lot of time.

When you acquire a new computer, keep your old computer and peripherals as backup.

Keep in mind that in spite of its advanced technology, the computer is still just a computer. It's not omnipotent. It's not human. It's just a machine. It has its limitations. Accept computers for the amazing tools they are, but don't give them power over you. A computer can't think. It can't make decisions. It can't contemplate. It can't understand. It doesn't have intuition or insight or consciousness. It's not capable of joy or love or forgiveness. It can't dream or hope. It can't watch the sun set. It can't laugh. It can't even smile. It can crash, and you can be sure it will do so at the most inopportune time. But it can't get up and walk away from you, as you can from it—at least not yet.

24. Use the Internet Consciously

One of the new ailments of the technological age is an addiction to being online. Obviously the Internet is a magnificent tool for research and can save us vast amounts of time. It also offers the potential for each of us to connect with every other person on the planet and thereby to achieve the oneness we're all seeking. The possibilities for that are truly mind-boggling. But according to research conducted at major universities around the country, for many people being online has become a time-wasting habit. For millions of others, it can be anything from a disturbing dependency to a compulsive disorder.

Addictive Internet use can include various activities, such as excessive e-mail use, Web surfing, online games, and time spent in chat rooms. At a minimum Net use can be a time-waster; at a maximum it's self-destructive. It can lead to fatigue, loss of productivity, decrease in the quality of work, loss of connection with coworkers, loss of sleep, and even loss of one's job.

Obviously, none of these results will simplify your work life. If you have a tendency to stay wired to the screen beyond the normal time required for your responsibilities, take whatever measures are necessary to keep your use within limits. Take frequent breaks, walk around the block, limit your access to the computer as much as possible. Identify work-oriented tasks you can do instead: Place phone calls, handle the mail, read, brainstorm on your own or with a coworker about an upcoming project. Be sure to refresh your energy by drinking a glass of water, doing some deep breathing, or thumping the thymus (#39).

Figure out how to best utilize this marvelous tool for your growth and evolution, but develop the will and the discipline to ensure that it doesn't rob you of your time and your life.

25. Learn to Make the Right Decisions Quickly

One sure sign of an effective worker is the ability to make good decisions quickly. For some this is an innate talent. For most, however, it's an acquired skill. Developing this ability will not only save you considerable amounts of time, but studies have shown that quick decisions are usually better decisions.

You can easily test this for yourself. For the next six months maintain a decisions journal in which you keep track of the decisions you make. Include everything from deciding if and how to make an important business phone call, to whether to attend an upcoming business conference, to deciding when and how to best ask for a raise, to deciding whether to accept a new position. With each decision, note how long it takes you to decide; then as time goes on, make notes about which decisions were appropriate for you and which ones, in hindsight, you'd now make differently.

Not only will you find that the decisions you make quickly

are the better ones, but also you'll find you're much happier and more confident with those than you are with the decisions you made using laborious analysis. The fact is, in most cases, you already know what you need to know to make the right decision.

The trick is learning to go with your first instinct. This is one good reason to eliminate as many of the distractions in your work life as possible. Often our days are so filled with unimportant minutiae that we easily get disconnected from our inner guidance. Once we clear out the clutter, it's so much easier to get connected and stay connected. But getting connected takes practice.

Years ago I learned a classic muscle-testing technique that rarely fails in helping me make good decisions quickly. It's based on the theory of applied kinesiology and utilizes the electromagnetic current in the body's energy field to give us information we can use effectively.

You can learn to use your body's energy field as well as your mind to help you make good decisions quickly. Here's a simple way to do that:

Stand up straight with both feet planted firmly on the ground. You can fold your arms casually across your chest; or you can bring your right hand to your solar plexus, put your left hand on top of your right hand, and hold them both gently to your body. Take a couple of deep, clearing breaths—in through the nose, out through the mouth. Then settle fully and comfortably into your stance. It helps in the beginning to close your eyes, not only to eliminate visual distractions but also to help you get in touch with your center.

First, you'll need to determine how your body responds in this exercise to a yes and how it responds to a no. For most people, a "yes" response will tilt the body slightly forward; a "no" response will tilt the body slightly backward. To determine how your body responds, simply ask your subconscious to give you a yes and to give you a no, and see which way you tilt with each.

Once you know this, ask yourself if it's truly in your best interest to take whatever action you may be considering. Take another deep breath, allowing your body to settle even more comfortably and solidly into your standing position. If the decision you've made is right for you, your body will start to fall forward ever so slightly; if the decision isn't right, your body will start to fall backward ever so slightly.

The more you work with this, the better you'll get. Eventually you'll be able to adapt this technique, if you choose, to a sitting position—at your desk, or in a business meeting. You'll reach the point where you can unobtrusively call upon your body's innate intelligence to help you make wise decisions. You'll also learn to get a sense about when you're not getting an accurate reading from this technique. Usually this happens either when you're not fully centered in your stance or when you allow your emotions to interfere. With practice and a strong intention, you'll learn to recognize the positive or negative effect your decision has on your energy field. This is one more way to put your subconscious mind to work for you, so you can work less.

26. Go Through the Doors

While the body-testing technique is a valuable tool, it may not work for every decision. You'll get a feel for when that technique will help you and when you may need to consider other methods. Here's another simple exercise that will help you save time when you need to choose between two or more options.

Find a quiet space where you won't be disturbed.

Close your eyes and breathe deeply for a moment or two.

Bring the two options clearly to mind. Let's say you're trying to decide whether to accept a promotion you've been offered by your current employer, Option A, or whether you should take a position you have been offered with another company, Option B.

Then imagine you're sitting at one end of a beautiful room. Sunshine is streaming through the windows. You're totally comfortable and at ease.

Look to the far end of the room and notice that there are

two closed doors there. One door is marked Option A. The other door is marked Option B.

Imagine yourself getting up from your chair and walking toward the door marked Option A. Notice how you feel as you approach that door. Do you feel good? Do you feel hesitant? If so, notice what is causing that hesitancy. When you reach the door, before you open it, stand at the door for a few moments. Here you are, about to accept Option A. In a moment you're going to walk through that door and accept the promotion you've been offered. Are you excited? Do you have a sense that this is the door you should be going through?

Now open the door and move fully into that option. You've accepted the promotion. How do you feel about it? How do you feel about your new boss? Is he or she someone you'll be happy working for? Will this position make it possible for you to do the work you want to do? Will it be a good stepping-stone for your future work? How do you feel about staying with this company? Are you proud to be a part of it? Will the work you'll now be doing help you make the contribution you want to make? How will taking this new position affect your family? Will you be able to keep your life in balance?

Walk farther through the door and see yourself six months from now, a year from now, five years from now. Employ all your senses (#36) to see if this is the next step your soul is calling to you to take.

When you feel complete, imagine yourself going back through that door and back to the chair at the far end of the room. Take a few deep breaths.

Now go through the same process with the door marked Option B.

You might want to make some notes about how each option made you feel and what questions you have. The chances are good that you'll get a strong feel for which option is the right one for you. Obviously, if you have another option or two, you can simply imagine other doors. For example, a third option in this situation might be to stay in the job you now have, and you could go through that door to get a sense of whether that is the best choice.

I often find that all I have to do is *think* of stepping through the door of one of the options I'm considering to get a clear idea of the right course of action. Sometimes just thinking about going through one of the doors is unappealing, which I hadn't realized until I began the exercise. As you get more adept at this process, you'll sense immediately which door to choose and which option is right for you.

THREE

Being More Productive

27. Eliminate the Distractions

Once you've cut back on the amount of time you work, you'll find you're automatically more productive. You'll be less stressed, more rested and refreshed, and your head will be clearer. It'll be easier for you to focus on the work at hand and to get more done. You'll also be more open to ways of working smarter rather than harder. In this part I describe a variety of techniques to help you get more work done in less time.

Begin by eliminating the distractions that throw you off schedule. For the next several days keep track of the ways you get sidetracked from your work, then think about ways you can minimize them. Here are some things to be aware of:

- Keep tempting videos, games, books, and other reading matter out of your office. If you work at home, you may need to keep them out of sight in other areas of your home. If you have computer games that are eating up more time than you care to admit, uninstall them.

- Keep all personal bills, correspondence, catalogs, and reading materials out of your work area.

- For business phone calls, as I've already discussed, set up regular times when people can phone you and when you can return calls, and mark that time off on your schedule each day. It's almost impossible to be productive and creative when you're constantly interrupted by a ringing phone.

- For personal phone calls, use common sense. Obviously there are times when you need to take care of personal business during your workday. If you frequently have to make personal calls, again, set aside a specific time each day to take care of them. Let your family, friends, and other associates know what that time is, and make sure they honor those times as much as possible.

- There's a time and place for office socializing, but if there are certain people in your work life who take up your time with trivial chitchat, figure out how to keep them from stopping by your office, or get them to move on quickly. Close your office door; put up a "Do Not Disturb" sign; assume a business posture that says "I'm busy and can't stop to talk now"; or simply come right out and say that you have work you need to complete by the end of the day. Stand up when someone comes into your office or your work space so you—and they—don't get settled in for a long chat that will take you away from the work you want to get done. Let the office gossips know that you don't have time to talk about others.

- If you have an assistant, let him know that minimizing distractions is important to you; train him to help you guard your time.

If you're constantly behind schedule, always staying late at the office, or taking work home, the chances are good it's the distractions that are keeping you from being productive.

28. Bring Your Full Attention to Your Work

No matter what you do, you won't be able to eliminate every single distraction. There'll always be something waiting in the wings to take you away from your work. But once you've eliminated most of the distractions, you can vastly improve your productivity by creating the conscious intention to fully concentrate on the task at hand.

You probably do this automatically when you're working to meet a specific deadline. You may be interrupted half a dozen times or more, but no matter what, you're able to refocus and to get the work completed on schedule. No doubt there are other times when you're less successful in getting back on track. Often this is why we take work home from the office or return to the office on weekends, when there are "no distractions."

Train yourself to have that concentrated focus during normal working hours, no matter how many people or distractions there are. When you come into your office or work space at the beginning of your workday—or whenever you start a new task—get into the habit of making the conscious decision to complete this task with your full attention and to make it as enjoyable as possible.

Take a deep breath, focus your energy, and consciously direct that powerful intention to the job at hand. With practice, you can actually feel your energy being focused in your body and your mind and being directed to your work. That's it. It's so simple yet so effective. The increase in productivity you'll experience is analogous to putting a piece of paper in the sunlight and hoping it will burn versus focusing sunlight with a magnifying glass so the paper will catch fire.

You can write "Focus!" on Post-it Notes and place them in strategic locations to remind you, or write "Attention!" in your day planner next to each project until you get into the habit of focusing automatically before you start each task. This practice will double your productivity.

29. Use a Timer

I have found a timer invaluable in keeping me on track and helping me do more in less time.

Ecko makes a timer that also functions as a stopwatch and is small enough to fit in your pocket. It runs forever on a battery the size of an aspirin. You can find a timer of this type in the kitchen utensil aisle in the supermarket, in a good hardware store, or in a variety store. Use an electronic timer rather than a wind-up timer that ticks; the ticking will drive you nuts.

Casio and others make wristwatches that include timers for around $25. Or your computer or PDA may have a built-in timer. Find a timer that suits your needs, and make it your alter ego on the job.

You can set it to remind you to make an important phone call.

You can set it to beep five minutes before you need to leave for an appointment so you won't be late or have to rush.

You can set it when you get a long-winded caller on the phone, to remind you—and the caller—that it's time to wrap up your conversation.

You can set it to remind you to daydream (#37), to wake you up from your ten-minute refresher nap (#38), to keep you on schedule for your walk around the block (#32), to police your time on the Net (#24), or to thump your thymus (#39) at 3 P.M. when your energy usually starts to lag.

You can set it to beep every half hour to get you into the habit of stopping to stretch or rub your shoulders or get up and move about so you'll avoid carpal tunnel problems.

You can use it to help your staff and coworkers stay on schedule in meetings.

You can use it to remind yourself to leave the office on time at the end of the day until you get into the habit of doing so on your own.

You can use a timer to remind you to focus your attention so you can cut in half the amount of time you need to finish a job. For example, if you've always given yourself a couple of hours to complete a certain task, set your timer for half that time just to see how much you can accomplish. You may not be able to cut the time in half on the first try, but if you keep at it, you'll let your subconscious mind know that you want to become more efficient at this particular job. It'll automatically come up with ways you can do that—ways that will seem obvious or even miraculous, but that you never would have thought of if you hadn't set that goal.

The idea here is not to put yourself under the stress of a clock. Rather, it's to use this tiny tool as a gentle reminder to begin or to get back to the task at hand. It will help you to learn to do more in less time, so you can leave your job at a reasonable hour—or even early—and begin to enjoy the rest of your life.

30. Take Your Lunch Break

Twelve years ago my friend Karen, a former landscape gardener, started her own retail business in which she sells beautiful, up-scale, often one-of-a-kind decorative landscape pieces such as fountains, birdbaths, statuary, lawn furniture, and the like. After ten years of working ten- and twelve-hour days five and six days a week, the business was finally doing well. But she confessed she was so exhausted she could barely think. Like many small retail business owners, she seldom took even a coffee break, let alone a lunch break, because that was often her busiest time. She felt she couldn't afford a full-time helper and she believed it would be impossible to find someone to fill in for her for just an hour midday. When I spoke with her two years ago, she was seriously considering letting go of the business.

I strongly urged her to look for someone to relieve her, not only for her lunch break, but for two to three hours beyond that at least three days a week. Then she could not only have her lunch time, but she could also use the additional time to handle paperwork, bills and ordering, which she usually had to stay late, after the store closed, to take care of.

With some trepidation, she followed my advice. She started taking her lunch breaks. She made sure she got away from the store so she could clear her head and get some fresh insights about where her business was going. After a while she began to realize that many of her customers could use her design expertise in arranging and planting their gardens and landscapes. Before long she had an active landscape-design consulting business two to three afternoons a week.

Not only did the consulting business keep her in closer touch with what her customers wanted so she could keep her store stocked accordingly, but she also loved the opportunity to be out in the fresh air using her creative design talents. And needless to say, the consulting business significantly improved her bottom line: She paid a part-time clerk $10 an hour and billed her services at $120 an hour.

By taking such a simple step as reclaiming her lunch break, she was able to step back a bit each day and gain a whole new perspective on her business.

Whether you work for yourself or someone else, when you fail to take your lunch break, you're working at least five hours more each week than you need to. It may not seem like all that much, but over the course of a year, it's the equivalent of working an extra month and a half. Over the course of ten years it's the equivalent of working an extra year.

Not only is it senseless to work that extra time, but when you routinely miss out on a break at midday you lose a priceless daily opportunity to restore your mind, your body, and your spirit. As anyone who engages in sports activities knows, taking regular breaks is a vital part of building endurance and achieving long-term success. The same principles apply to work.

If your business life requires you to regularly have lunch with clients and other associates, don't delude yourself into thinking that because you're having lunch in these situations that you're taking a break. You're still working, and you need a break from that work to help you stay focused and productive. Whenever you schedule a luncheon meeting, write in some additional time on your schedule for your own break. Taking even fifteen minutes for a walk or even a brief nap can make a big difference in what you're able to accomplish during the rest of the day.

31. When You're in Overwhelm, Stop

It doesn't happen too often anymore, but awhile back I found myself completely inundated with work. I'd unthinkingly committed myself to too many deadlines because I'd failed to double my estimate, and they were all staring me in the face. I had five days in which to complete several projects that would take me at least two weeks. I was overwhelmed and simply didn't know how I could possibly get everything completed on time. You've likely been in that kind of situation, so you know it feels as if you can't stop, even to get a bite to eat.

But because I've done it before, I knew what I had to do to get everything completed on time: I took the day off. I left my office, my computer, and a ringing phone early in the morning and went for a nice long walk on the beach. I found a little bakery and had a piping hot triple decaffeinated mocha with whipped cream, which I nursed until it was time for lunch. Then I enjoyed the luncheon special in a new little café. Later, because

it was so deliciously self-indulgent, I watched the matinee showing of a movie I'd been waiting to see. On the way home, I
stopped in a community garden and delighted in the birds and
the setting sun. I went home for dinner, watched a favorite video,
and went to bed. I didn't spend a moment of that time thinking
consciously about all the things that were hanging over my head.
But I knew my subsconscious mind would be working in my
absence, and I did boot it up (#40) when I went to sleep that
night.

When I got up the next morning, I had complete clarity
about what I needed to do over the next few days in order to
finish everything on time. I started in with a freshness and a
vigor I hadn't had for weeks and got each of the projects completed. I even ended up with a free afternoon on the last day.

I know this sounds crazy, but it works. The next time you
find yourself overwhelmed, stop. Take the entire day (use a sick
day, a vacation day, a personal day, or whatever), and create your
own version of not working. You won't believe how it will empower you.

32. Walk Around the Block

I realize there's an off chance you won't believe me about stopping in your tracks for an entire day when you're overwhelmed by having too much to do. If that's the case, then don't take the entire day. Take a ten-minute walk instead.

The moment you realize things are out of control, stand up, leave your office just as it is, and walk out the door without saying anything to anyone. (You won't be gone long enough for anyone to miss you, and if you say something to someone you run the risk of getting sidetracked.) If it's raining, take your umbrella, but leave your pens, paper, day planner, cell phone, notebook, and everything else behind.

Walk briskly for ten minutes as if you had nothing else in the world to do. Breathe deeply as you walk, and get your heart pumping. Notice the temperature of the air. If it's hot, feel the heat. If it's cold, feel the cold. If it's windy, feel the wind in your hair. Observe the sky, the clouds, the trees. Be aware of the traffic, the people, the lights, the sounds. Live for these ten minutes as if nothing else matters in the world but this walk and what you're experiencing in these moments. Whatever you do, don't allow your mind to worry about what's going on back in the office—though you can give it all a little inner smile (#33).

When the ten minutes are up, go back to the office. Notice the difference in the way you feel and the fresh approach and the new energy you can bring to the tasks that are waiting for you. If this works, next time you may have the courage to take the whole day. If it doesn't work, it may be because what you *need* is the whole day.

There are significant benefits to taking a break like this. The fresh air and the deep breathing clear your head and send new energy to your brain. The cardiovascular benefit of walking briskly while breathing deeply refreshes both your circulatory system and your psyche. In addition, the sunlight, the contact with nature, and the change of scene all help to give you a new perspective. The more you take advantage of this kind of break when you're in overwhelm, the more obvious the benefits will be.

You'll see that taking a breather not only reduces your stress, it vastly enhances your productivity. You'll also learn to distinguish between the times when a ten-minute refresher walk will do the trick and the times when you need to stop for a day or more. I grant that in the beginning, it may take a monumental leap of faith for you to walk away in the midst of chaos and pressing deadlines, but you'll soon see how much more productive you can be when you return. And the more breaks you take, the less often you'll find yourself overwhelmed.

33. Work with an Inner Smile

Scientific studies have revealed that when we smile, endorphins are released in the brain. Smiling creates an instantaneous, safe, and completely natural "high." We can use those endorphins to our benefit in the workplace. One simple way to do that is to learn the art of the inner smile.

This doesn't mean you'll be walking around with a silly grin or a phony smile on your face. Rather, it's about learning to smile inwardly in a way that's not particularly noticeable to anyone else but has a powerful effect on your ability to bring a positive state to any problem, challenge, or interaction.

An inner smile is a gentle radiation of confident, pleasant energy. The endorphins cause your physiology to relax while at the same time making you mentally alert. Every time you engage in this inner smile you connect with your soul.

Try it right now. Think of something you truly love—your own little sloop sailing into the sunset, the face of a baby, a hole in one, birds flitting about at your backyard feeder, your kids playing happily together—anything that makes you smile. But don't let the smile actually appear. Just feel that smiling energy inwardly. Your lips may curve up slightly, your eyes may shine with a slight twinkle, but you're not visibly smiling. Keep it within.

Now notice the difference the endorphins make in your body. Your whole being feels lighter and more energized. Experience the euphoria. Watch how quickly it can change how you feel. Strengthen that euphoria by concentrating on it, and practice sustaining it.

Now think of a minor problem you're dealing with at work. Take one minute and smile with that inner smile at the problem. Then notice how much more centered you are and how more solvable that problem seems.

You can use an inner smile in countless situations to relieve tension and reduce the stress that automatically builds up in your normal workday. Use it when you're caught in traffic on the way to work in the morning, or when your kids are running late and you can't get them out the door. Use it when your boss or a coworker snaps at you, when you've misplaced an important document, or when you just found out that the shipment you were expecting today won't be delivered until next week.

Once you've incorporated inner smiles into your day, you'll develop a clarity about everyday problems you haven't had before. You'll nip problems in the bud and get along better with your coworkers. And you'll develop unique solutions and intuitive insights into the daily challenges of the workplace that will help you be more productive.

34. Laugh Right Out Loud

I recently acquired a new computer, which, like many products these days, hadn't been thoroughly tested before it was shipped to me. I worked with the manufacturer's tech support and my own consultants for over two months trying to get this ill-conceived and inadequately inspected piece of machinery to do the bare minimum of what I needed it to do, which is word processing. It crashed every other day, leaving me stranded and unable to work.

Needless to say, this was frustrating in the extreme. In times past I'd have been sorely tempted to throw the darn thing through the window. But fortunately in recent years I've learned to laugh. There were moments during this trying period when my ability to laugh saved my sanity. If you've dealt with the downside of modern technology, you know what I mean. There are times that are so seemingly defeating that the only thing you can do is laugh, cry, or go nuts. It's far simpler to laugh.

So here's what I did. Every time the technological gremlins achieved a victory, I pushed myself back from my desk and laughed right out loud. I often had to begin with a pretend full-belly laugh. This invariably led to a genuine full-body laugh, which, from practice, I can easily keep going for several minutes, or as long as I need to. Then I could go back to the computer with a clearer perspective and the patience to figure out what I needed to do to get it working again.

You can do this, too. Even when you start with a fake laugh, laughing propels you to another dimension, and you can begin to see the cosmic humor that is always just the other side of frustration. And when you work at it, the true laugh follows. Laughing changes the endorphins in your body, clears the air, relaxes your physical as well as your emotional and mental bodies, and brings new insight to whatever situation you're facing. Laughing makes it possible for you to come back to the problem at hand with a fresh approach, minus the upset.

You can use laughter in any number of situations, on your own or with others. I regularly meet with a group of business associates. Before we start our meeting we spend several minutes laughing. Laughing is infectious and can completely change the energy in a room so that everyone feels good. It's a powerful way to start or end a meeting, or to help you recover from an angry client or a rude customer. It's a great way to start a meal or to end a meal, or to start your day or to end your day. And often it's good simply to sit back and laugh for no reason at all.

Of course, people may question your sanity while you're laughing to save it, but don't let that bother you; keep 'em guessing as to why you're so much more centered and productive now that you know how to laugh right out loud.

35. Stop Procrastinating

The habit of procrastinating wreaks havoc with our work schedules and with the time it takes to complete a project, not to mention the quality of our work and the way we feel about it. Basically we procrastinate for any one or a combination of these four reasons:

1. We do it, unconsciously, to challenge ourselves. Every time we procrastinate we get an opportunity to see that we can actually force ourselves to complete a task in much less time than we had consciously anticipated. It adds a level of excitement to our lives.

2. Perfectionists procrastinate because it lets them off the hook. They can convince themselves and usually others that the results of their hard work would have been much better if they'd had more time. Also, a perfectionist can get another level of praise: "Gee, if you did this well in such a short time, imagine what you could have done if you'd had

all the time you needed." This can provide a boost to your self-esteem and even make you feel good about procrastinating.

3. Many people procrastinate out of the fear of failure. If we took all the time available and we did a lousy job, then we'd have no excuse— we're just failures. But if we can make it appear that the job is a failure because we didn't have enough time, we can somehow convince ourselves, and anyone else who's paying attention, that if we'd had time, we could've done it right.

4. Other people procrastinate out of the fear of success. If we take all the time we need and succeed beautifully, then we may have to face the fact that we're capable and competent. If we've got programming from our past that says we're just average, then succeeding is contrary to our sense of self, and that can be uncomfortable. Or perhaps we have an unconscious fear that if we succeed, we'll make someone else—a parent or a boss—look bad. Or if we succeed, we might have to admit that we could have been succeeding all along, and perhaps our lives have been wasted.

If you find that you regularly procrastinate, you could greatly improve the quality of your work life by becoming conscious of your pattern and training yourself to think differently.

For example, you could make a point of taking on work and projects that are true challenges for you. Set up your work life and your work schedule so you're forced to utilize all of your talents to complete a task and still have time and energy left over for the other parts of your life.

You could make the conscious decision that you won't allow yourself to feel good about the secondary praise that comes from doing a good job in half the time. Simply let go of that false ego stroking and don't be uplifted by it. Instead, learn to derive a sense of worth from truly doing the best you can, knowing that if you choose, you can get better and better.

You could realize that becoming perfect is an ultimate goal you're going to spend the rest of your life achieving. Relax and let that striving for perfection be part of the beauty of your growth process.

Understand the fundamental truth that there's no such thing as failure. A failure is just a learning experience on the way to accomplishing your goal. As long as you don't quit, it's impossible to fail.

Let go of the effect your success has on other people. The truth is that when you claim your own power, you become an inspiring model to others. Refuse to take responsibility for the way someone else reacts to your success. When you take on a project, do it because you want to do it, and let go of anyone else's reaction to your outcome.

You can also use your timer to help you stop procrastinating. Set it to go off in five minutes, or in half an hour, or at noon, or whenever. When the timer beeps, it's time to start working. If you bring your full attention to this (#28), you'll train your subconscious mind to get ready by generating positive energy and new ideas for the work you'll be doing.

Reward yourself for not procrastinating. Every time you force yourself to jump right in and wrap up a project, make a point of giving yourself a payoff commensurate with the task to honor your commitment to break the procrastination habit.

36. Employ All Your Senses

Part of what we're trying to do in learning to be more productive is to make our work lives more fun, more exciting, more enjoyable. At the same time we want to cut back on the amount of time we spend working so we can keep our lives in better balance. We want to eliminate the exhaustion and the drudgery of overwork and put our underutilized resources to work for us in ways we haven't done before. Learning to use all your senses is a good way to do that.

Our experience of life comes through our five senses. Each sense gives us specific and useful information about our physical world. Imagine for a moment that you didn't have the sense of smell. How much less rich your world would be. In our mostly traditional work culture we act as if we have only one sense, either visual or auditory. Most of us are trained to use one of these two senses as our dominant sense, to the exclusion of our other senses.

Here is one approach you can use to start utilizing your other senses when faced with an opportunity, a conflict, a potential problem, or a challenge in the workplace.

Start by figuring out what your dominant sense is. Do you see the situation in your mind's eye, then move things around spatially in order to understand it? Do you hear input, then think it through? Whichever sense you normally use, know that you can multiply it by five to vastly increase your ability to work at your maximum capacity while minimizing the time you have to spend working. When you know your dominant sense, use it first to analyze the situation.

Now pick another sense you can use in addition to your dominant sense. For example, once you've analyzed the situation from your usual audio sense, switch to the visual mode. No more talking out loud or verbalizing the circumstances. Force yourself to visualize a solution.

Next use the sense of touch and notice how the situation feels in your body and where it shows up. Do you feel it in your gut? In your head? In your heart? Move the problem around to various parts of your body and note how the people, the events, the possibilities feel. Do you feel good about the solution you've come up with? Or do you get an uncomfortable feeling? You can use this feeling to help you decide on a course of action.

Then use your sense of taste. How does this situation taste in your mouth? Try this right now. Take a moment to think of a situation that you've been considering with your dominant sense, and notice the taste sensation in your mouth. You might get a sweet wonderful taste. Or you could get a taste that is rancid or metallic or otherwise unappealing. This is valuable information you can use.

Then use your sense of smell. When all other systems fail and you're unable to decide what to do, smell it. Try this right now. Think about a course of action you're taking that you're not certain about and simply smell it. It may smell sweet or pleasant. Or you may get a sour smell that makes you turn up your nose and say "Yuk!" or "I smell a rat." Keep smelling until you're clear about what that smell means. You'll get some new information about this situation that you hadn't considered before.

Each sense uses a completely different pathway to the brain. By using all your senses in the workplace, you'll be accessing more of your brain power. When you put all your senses to work, you can work less.

37. Daydream with Intention

We all engage in spontaneous pauses throughout the day. We can be working at something and then, without being consciously aware of it, we zone out. We come back twenty seconds later and we're right back where we were, unaware that we've been gone.

These pauses are necessary for our psychic health. So the goal here is not to eliminate them but rather to use them to be more productive. Get into the habit of generating these spontaneous pauses consciously, and learn to utilize them for a specific purpose.

One way to do this is to focus on a question or problem related to your work. Pose a question to your subconscious mind with a strong expectation that you'll get an answer. Then relax and allow yourself to daydream, letting your mind wander wherever it goes. After several minutes you may have an answer. Or it may seem as if nothing at all has happened, then the next afternoon a solution will come to you. You'll still be getting the daydreaming you need, but you'll be doing it in a way that is supporting your work.

Another way to use these breaks is to sit back, set your timer, relax, and let your mind wander, with the intention that you'll feel refreshed and centered and clear at the end of the daydream. If you do this consciously, you won't need to take a nap (#38).

We know that Einstein found daydreaming vital for his work. Many companies now actively encourage employees to use a portion of their time thinking or dreaming about ways to improve their products or services. 3-M, for example, developed a 15 percent rule, which encourages their technical staff to spend up to 15 percent of their work time on projects of their own choosing—thinking, wondering about, and daydreaming to come up with solutions to ideas that are near and dear to their hearts. That's how 3-M employee Art Fry developed Post-it Notes.

Just imagine what problems of the world could be solved if we all learned to daydream effectively.

38. Take a Nap

If you're like most people, you work at your maximum efficiency for the first hour or two of your workday, then your efficiency slowly dwindles. By the time 2 P.M. rolls around, you're functioning at 40 percent of your capacity.

This means you're only half as effective from ten to noon as you are from nine to ten. Then if you take a lunch break at noon, presumably you able to work at closer to your maximum efficiency until roughly three, when your efficiency drops again. The result is you're losing three to four hours of your peak efficiency every single day.

But there's a way to work at your maximum efficiency for close to eight hours each day. The body has access to the perfect system for totally rejuvenating itself in a very short period of time. It's called sleep. So all we need to do when we notice our energy is lagging is take a ten-minute nap.

The wonderful thing about naps is that they make it possible for us to work better without having to take drugs such as coffee or caffeinated teas or sodas.

If your work environment allows, get a blanket and one of those roll-up pads people use for aerobics and yoga classes and keep them in your office. When it's time to take a break, turn off the phone, put a "Do Not Disturb" sign on the door, and set your timer or watch for ten minutes. Then roll out your mat and zonk out. Lie on your back, feet together, hands on the floor close to your body so all your energy is contained. Your body will be using energy for rejuvenation rather than for keeping you warm, so it's helpful to cover yourself with the blanket. You want to minimize the possibility of getting chilled, which would make it impossible for you to relax completely. In those ten minutes you can bring yourself back up to your morning's energy level.

If you're not getting enough sleep, it'll be hard to recharge in ten minutes. If you're sleep deprived or have had a bad night's sleep, you might be better off sleeping for an hour. Your drive then returns, and your energy will be back up to your maximum level. Even if it takes an hour to recharge, you'll still be better off than if you keep pressing on when you're exhausted, working at less than half your normal level of efficiency.

39. Give Yourself a Thump

Unfortunately, though things are changing rapidly, not every office has a work culture that encourages naps. If napping is frowned upon in your work environment, get into the habit of using three thumps as a quick and powerful way to energize yourself whenever you're feeling drowsy, have difficulty concentrating, or find your energy is lagging.

I learned this technique from Donna Eden, author of *Energy Medicine* (Tarcher/Putnam, 1998). Donna, in my opinion, is one of the great intuitive healers of our time. For over twenty years she has been teaching people how to tap into the body's energy system to generate healing and to enhance physical vitality and mental acuity. Based on the theory that the body is designed to heal itself, energy medicine employs, among other systems, your body's energy pathways, called meridians, that have been used in acupuncture for thousands of years. Meridians can be used in predictable ways to positively affect your energy field.

Start by thumping your K-27 meridians, which are located about one inch below and to the outside of your collarbone. Using the fingers of both hands, or the thumb and index finger of one hand, find the slight indentation in that area, and tap or massage these points firmly for about twenty seconds. Breathe deeply, in through your nose and out through your mouth, while you're tapping.

Next, move one hand to your thymus, located in the center of your chest, several inches below your K-27 points. Firmly tap your thymus for about twenty seconds while breathing deeply, in through your nose and out through your mouth.

Then thump your spleen meridian points. To do this, move your hands to six inches on either side of the thymus and down to find the slight indentation between your first and second rib. Firmly tap with several fingers for about twenty seconds on your spleen meridians, while breathing deeply, in through your nose and out through your mouth.

As you can see, this exercise takes approximately one minute. You can do one or more of the thumps while sitting at your desk, in the middle of observing an important presentation when your body wants nothing more than to fall into a deep sleep, or at any other time when you need an immediate energy fix. If you don't have time to thump all three of these meridian centers, take just twenty seconds and thump your K-27 points for an emergency energy booster. (Don't worry about what others will think if they see you tapping your K27s during a meeting. One of two things might happen: You could start a trend so that everyone you work with would learn how to instantly boost their energy levels; or you could find that you're invited to fewer meetings, which would greatly simplify your work life.)

Not only does this series of taps instantly raise your energy level, it strengthens your immune system and also improves your coordination and balance. It'll make it possible for you to think much more clearly and will vastly increase your productivity. I've found it so effective that I incorporated it into my early-morning routine every day. And I automatically use it during the day when I notice my energy is down or when I feel sleepy and don't want to take time for a nap. Try it right now so you can become familiar with the meridian points, and notice how it gives you an instant energy boost.

To learn more about energy medicine, I recommend you get Donna's six-hour video program, *Energy Healing with Donna Eden*. It's available through Innersource for $59.95 (800-835-8332). This tape series is exceptional. Not only will it show you many other techniques to reduce stress and increase your energy levels, but it will also teach you literally dozens of simple processes you can use in a multitude of health-enhancing ways. I believe energy medicine is the medicine of the future. I don't know of a better way you could spend sixty dollars to achieve immediate and long-term health benefits. The program also will help you build a repertoire of techniques you can use every day to enhance your energy and to improve your productivity.

40. Put Your Subconscious Mind
to Work for You

We often get so caught up in using our modern technology that we forget that we have a wide array of inner technologies to help us. One vast, mostly untapped reservoir of time just waiting to be utilized is our sleep time. Roughly one-third of our lives is spent in sleep, yet most people don't use that time as effectively as they could. We go to sleep without clearing out the clutter of the day and end up tossing and turning or having disturbing dreams. Without our being aware of it, poor sleep adversely affects the quality of our work.

Here is a simple process you can use every night of the week to assist you in tapping into that subconscious part of you that sees the greater purpose in your life.

1. Before you go to sleep, take three minutes to review your day. Bring to mind anything from the day that is still unresolved or causing you

grief—an argument with a coworker, a looming deadline, a new project you're unsure how to begin.

2. Then take a moment or two to imagine the situation being resolved in a positive way or to come to a feeling of completion or an inner knowing that the circumstances will unfold to the best advantage of everyone involved. Just accept that your subconscious mind sees the greater purpose and knows intuitively how the part you're playing fits into the whole in a positive and life-affirming way.

3. Then make a request to your subconscious mind that you'll wake up in the morning with an understanding about how to proceed. You may find it helpful to write out your request in a sleep journal, which you can keep next to your bed. Simply ask your subconscious mind to resolve the situation for you while you have a great night's sleep.

4. In the morning, when you first wake up, pick up your journal and begin writing as if you knew the answer. You could jump-start the response by writing something like "What I need to do now in this situation is . . ." and just trust that the response will flow. Keep writing until it does.

You can do this every night to establish a rapport with that inner part of you that knows all the answers. Your subconscious mind is like an employee who is available to work around the clock. You just have to let it know what you want it to do. You'll soon find that you don't want to make any decision or start any project without the help and guidance of your subconscious mind.

Realize that there's no end to the different kinds of help you can get from this source and that the more you use it, the better it gets. You can ask specific questions to which you will receive specific answers. You can request that you get a resolution to a relationship issue or insight to a health problem. You can get guidance on how to begin a project, the best way to ask for a raise, how to deal with your employees. When you ask for help, make sure your requests relate to your own life and are life enhancing.

With this process you can improve the quality of your work life overnight. And you'll find that you can relax about your work and even work less because your subconscious is working more.

For many other delightful ways to use this incredible technology, read my friend Henriette Anne Klauser's book, *Write It Down, Make It Happen* (Scribner, 2000). This enchanting book will give you dozens of ways to use your subconscious mind to help you achieve your goals.

41. Get a Life

One of the things we're trying to achieve in simplifying our work lives is balance. Having a well-balanced life can greatly add to both the quality and quantity of the work you do.

How long has it been since you were able to take time to contribute to your community in a meaningful way?

When was the last time you did something besides recycling that was significant for the environment?

How long has it been since you created the opportunity to be with friends and enjoy their company, or were able to spend time helping someone you know through a crisis?

Have you been able to take the time in recent years to be in touch with relatives outside of your immediate family?

Do you regularly create the opportunity to spend time in nature?

Do you long to be involved in theater or the arts but never have the time?

Are you able to devote an appropriate amount of time to maintaining a healthy diet and a high level of physical fitness?

Do you have a hobby you enjoy, and do you devote adequate time to it?

Do you routinely get enough sleep?

Do you have emotional issues that could or should be addressed through professional counseling sessions if only you had the time?

Do you regularly meditate or pray or do anything that would fulfill your aspiration to have more spirituality in your life?

When was the last time you actually had fun?

When we spend all our time working, we lose our connection with the outside world. Our lives can easily become lackluster and lose meaning. There's a reason the old saying "All work and no play makes Jack a dull boy" is still around.

FOUR

Being More Effective with People

42. Speak Up

You may be good at saying no in other areas of your life, but if you don't know how to say no in the workplace, not only does it complicate your life at work but also it can adversely affect the rest of your life as well. Your failure to say no when it's appropriate carries a high price. It wastes time, creates stress, causes you to become overextended, erodes your productivity, damages your self-esteem, and diminishes the special contribution only you can make. When you learn to set good boundaries, you'll come into your own. That's where you find and accomplish your true work.

In many office interactions it often seems easier just to keep your mouth shut and to keep on keeping on; and sometimes that's the right thing to do. But bear in mind that silence implies consent or agreement. In most cases, you simply have to learn to *speak* your truth. That's the only effective way to let other people know where you stand. Angry looks, slamming doors, cold shoulders, icy stares, and avoidance don't work. On the contrary, those kinds of ploys exacerbate the problem. People don't get the hint, or they can easily choose not to. When you speak up, your voice cannot be ignored. Obviously this doesn't mean you should scream or shout. As your mother probably told you, you can attract more flies with honey than with vinegar. But that honey can't be sticky sweet; it has to be strongly laced with your own clear understanding of what you want.

You and you alone are responsible for letting someone else know where you stand. No one else can do that for you. If you approach your work with the conscious intention to set appropriate limits, you'll soon learn how to pick your battles; how to develop the right tone so you're neither too harsh nor too meek; and how to set limits that are not too little, too late, or too often. With practice you can develop tact and timing, poise and dignity. Your ultimate goal is to learn how to set your boundaries in such a way that the statement of your truth in almost any situation has no more emotional charge than if you were commenting on the weather, but it gets your message across and sets you free. In this part we'll look at some ways you can set appropriate boundaries and make the most of your work relationships.

43. Learn These Boundary-setting Guidelines

If you approach boundary setting as a game or as a skill you need to learn to be better at what you do and to enhance the contribution you make, you automatically dispel much of the fear or dread that can surround this challenge.

Here are some general guidelines, which can be adapted to a variety of boundary-setting situations you'll find in the workplace.

1. Pick your approach carefully. There's no need to come on like a Mack truck when a simple "No, thanks" will do.

2. Until you're secure in your ability to set appropriate boundaries, take some time to consider your response. In a non-urgent, non-confrontational setting, you can simply say, "Let me get back to you later on this." In a heated encounter that could be explosive, give yourself at least overnight to develop the right approach.

3. Come up with an appropriate response you'd like to make, then practice it over and over again until it's a part of you. You want to be totally secure in your ability to carry through. If possible, role play with a friend, coworker, or family member. Or practice in front of the mirror and get into a new psychic groove of setting appropriate boundaries. See yourself as a person who's learned how to do this.

4. Once you have a plan and a response you're at ease with, take three to five minutes or more to laugh out loud (#34). Sometimes you get so wrought up about a situation that you can't think straight; laughing will help dispel any negative charge connected with this situation and may give you new insights.

5. Figure out the best- and the worst-case scenarios so you're prepared no matter what happens and so you know what your bottom line is. Let's say you always have a difficult time saying no to your boss when she asks you to stay late to finish up a project, even though you've told her you must leave by 5 P.M. to be home for your kids. The best-case scenario might be that she immediately agrees with you. The worst-case scenario might be that she has a screaming fit and tells you if you refuse to do the work, you're fired. If that's a possibility, you need to figure out your next step. Do you stand your ground and get fired? Do you back down for the moment, then look for another job?

Do you lobby for a reasonable compromise? Think it through carefully, and practice various scenarios so you're prepared.

6. Decide on the right time and place. You want to avoid a public confrontation and you want to be sure you have the other person's full attention. "Susan, I'd like to talk with you about my workload. Is this a good time, or would you prefer to set an appointment for later today?"

7. Just before you go in for the kill, take a couple of long, slow, deep breaths and "zip up" your central meridian (#49). When you have the floor, use a neutral voice, and play to her best side. Remember that people generally respond to you with the same tone you use with them.

8. Take a powerful stance—either sitting squarely or standing firmly on both feet—and make direct eye contact. If this is a challenge for you, be sure you practice ahead of time. Your position will be strengthened a thousandfold if you can look the person directly in the eye, state your case, and stand firm with it. If you fidget, shuffle your feet, and stare at the ceiling, you won't have a prayer of being taken seriously.

9. Make your request without belaboring it, then ask for a response: "Susan, I love working here and I want to do the best job for you I

possibly can, but I'm unable to work beyond five o'clock on a regular basis. I'd like for us to work together to set up a schedule so that I can get done what needs to get done. Are you willing to work with me on this?"

10. If you need some extra time to respond to a scenario you did not anticipate, don't be afraid to ask for it. "Let me think about that and I'll get back to you. Will nine o'clock tomorrow morning work for you?"

11. Whether you win or lose this round, always take the time afterward to analyze your performance. Figure out what worked and what didn't. This is one way to be certain that you'll perform even better next time. And there'll always be a next time.

44. Figure Out Why You Say Yes

You may find it helpful to understand why you often agree to demands on your time when you know you need to say no. You probably say yes for any one or a combination of the following reasons:

Like most of us, you were brought up to be agreeable, and you believe saying no means you're not an agreeable person.

You have an innate desire to help other people.

You were taught that it's more politic to get on the bandwagon than it is to decline to join in.

You were taught not to question authority.

You don't stop to figure out if you actually have the time to do it, or you agree to a request before you take the time to figure out whether you actually want to do it.

It almost always seems easier to agree to do it than it does to come up with a reason or an excuse not to.

You're afraid that if you say no, you'll never get another chance to prove that you have the talent, ability, skill, creativity, or intelligence to do it.

You're afraid that if you say no you'll be fired.

There's some part of you that wants to do it, even when the rest of you knows it's not possible, and in certain situations that part of you wins out.

Take a moment now to figure out if there are any other reasons you tend to respond in the affirmative. Then take the time to reframe each reason.

For example, when you stop to think about it you can easily see that saying no doesn't necessarily mean that you're not an agreeable person. If you're up-front about what you can and cannot do, people will honor that.

Also, the chances are slim, for example, that you'd actually get fired, especially if you're a capable and effective worker. The reaction of the person you're turning down will depend to a great extent on how you state your position. You can imagine the response you'd get if you got angry or upset or defensive and said, "How can you possibly ask me to do that? You *know* I don't have time. It's unreasonable for you to expect me to do this on top of everything else I have to do!" And you can also imagine a very different reaction if you calmly and graciously said, "Gee, I'd love to help you on that, but I just don't have the time right now. Perhaps we could get George to help, or can we figure out another way to get it done?"

Taking the time to examine the difficulty you have in saying no will give you the information you need to set appropriate limits. And remember, people naturally tend to take advantage of someone who can't say no. When you establish yourself as a person who sets reasonable boundaries, people will be much less likely to impose on you.

45. Ask People Not to Ask You
Before They Ask You

One way to maintain your boundaries is to head people off at the pass. Once you've decided what you want or how you need to spend your time and energy, let your boss, coworkers, friends, and family know. Ask them not to distract you or put you under additional pressure by asking you to do things you don't have time to do.

For example, if you've taken on a project at work that will consume a good deal of your attention for the next few months, you can simply let people know what you will and won't be able to do. "Now that I've started this project, I won't have time to be involved in the quarterly meetings or in the preparations for the annual company picnic. So don't even think about asking me!"

When you meet someone coming down the hall who you know is intent on dragooning you into being chairman of the intercity corporate spelling bee, beat him to the punch. Quickly smile your inner smile, then hold up your hand and say, "Bob, I know you're looking for someone to chair the bee, but count me out. I can't take on another assignment until I finish this one."

Before you accept a new obligation in your current job, let your boss know exactly what you'll be able to do and what other work will be affected. "If I take on this new sales campaign, I won't be able to also handle the human resources project we talked about. Do you want me to drop that, or can we get Joe to take that on until I've wrapped this up?"

When we fail to spell out our parameters ahead of time, false expectations can easily develop. This creates stress, exhaustion, resentment, poor work performance, and even illness, and it makes it so much harder to set the boundaries we want. But when the people you work with honor and respect the contribution you make, they'll respect your boundaries, as well, as long as you make them clear ahead of time and keep them clear as you go along.

We need to give ourselves—and others—the space to think, to grow, to create, and to achieve our full potential. Setting boundaries will help you do that for yourself and will set the example for others who need to do that, too.

46. Work Effectively with Your Boss

Eighty percent of your boss's satisfaction with you is related to only 20 percent of the work you perform. Your first task in learning to be as effective as possible is to find out what that 20 percent is. Then be certain that you put your attention on that 20 percent.

If you spend the majority of your time and energy on the 80 percent your boss doesn't care about, you're losing the opportunity to get the most out of your workday. You're also generating more stress for you and your boss and creating a mediocre impression that will only make your job harder and more time-consuming in the long run.

How do you find out what that 20 percent is? Ask. Whenever you start a new job, ask your employer to describe what he'd consider the ideal employee in your position. How would the employee perform? What attribute would make that employee the most valuable to him? Ask what tasks or area of the job you should most concentrate on. Then ask what the next most important area is, and then the next most important after that.

Do the same when you take on a new assignment in the job you already have. Make sure you know what your boss wants and expects so you can spend your time delivering that rather than something else entirely.

You may think the answers to these questions would be obvious, but if you went to three different bosses with the same questions, you'd get three different lists. You want to be certain you're not concentrating on the 20 percent your last boss thought most important.

In the beginning you may have to learn to read between the lines. When a project is completed, ask for feedback. What worked? What didn't? Is there anything the boss would like you to do differently next time? Be sure to take notes, which you can refer back to while you're completing the next project.

You can also use notes when the project is completed and your boss has inexplicably changed his mind. With good notes, you can say, "When we talked last Monday, you asked me to start on the fall catalog. Would you like me to focus on the sales meeting now instead?" Obviously you don't want to do this to set a trap or even to cover your tail, but in a genuine effort to understand what is expected of you. The boss may have forgotten what he asked for, or he may have changed his mind without letting you know. If he knows you're taking him at his word and sincerely trying to provide what he wants, the chances are better that he'll be more explicit to begin with or keep you informed as his needs and expectations change.

One of the most important steps you can take to reduce the pressure you put on yourself is to avoid making promises you can't keep that will throw the rest of your life out of balance. So if your boss asks when you expect to have a particular project completed, never, ever answer on the spot. Always respond with "Let me figure it out and I'll get back to you." Then actually take the time to realistically estimate, given your other duties, when you could have the project completed. Then double that estimate (#15).

Or, if the boss gives you a date that is unrealistic considering what else he has asked you to do, make sure he understands that other things won't get done. Find out what other responsibilities he wants you to let slide until this project is finished.

47. Work Effectively with Your Staff

Here are some ideas to help you get the most from the people who work for you.

- Make sure you let your employees know the 20 percent of the work on which they should be spending 80 percent of their time.
- When you assign a project, make sure your staff has a clear understanding of what you want so they don't end up wasting their time and yours producing something else.
- When you assign tasks to others and have given clear instructions, give them the freedom to complete the task without constantly looking over their shoulders. This creates trust and reduces stress—theirs and yours.
- Praise an employee who has done a good job. This instills the desire to do an even better job next time. Studies have shown that there is a dramatic increase in performance when praise immediately follows completion of the work.

- Respect the boundaries your employees set regarding the amount of time they can work.

- Demand and expect that your employees will do their best, and when they do, give them the one thing we all want—time off from time to time—as a special reward. This will give them a chance to recharge and help ensure that they'll continue to do their best.

- Own up to your role as boss, while seeing and treating your employees as equal human beings.

- Make sure you understand your company's worker-friendly policies and that you support your staff in taking advantage of them.

- One of the most effective ways you can empower staff members to work at their best is to recognize and acknowledge their inherent worth as individuals and their latent potential. See them as strong, noble, happy, creative, and productive. They'll live up to that image.

48. Work Effectively with Your Peers

Here's how to create an enjoyable work atmosphere and make the best use of the time you spend working with others.

- When you're collaborating with one or more coworkers on a project, make a point of working with them to create a common vision that you can all aim toward. Get an agreement from every member of the team as to exactly what you want to accomplish. While you may not all see exactly eye to eye, make sure that everyone is on board as far as possible. If someone in the group isn't in agreement with the team, make a point of drawing her out. Ask her questions, get her input and, ultimately, her agreement to work toward the common goal. You can waste your own and everyone else's time if you're not all on the same track.

- Make a practice of looking out for your coworkers, whether you're working with them or are in a competitive situation, such as in a sales environment. Be alert to ways you might be able to help someone else get their job done more easily. For example, you may be doing research and come across information someone else on the team could benefit from. Pass that information along and help her out. You'll create positive energy between you, and most people will naturally want to help you in return. Not only does this type of support pay off in practical ways, but it helps to create a more cooperative and productive work environment.

- Always be open to learning from others about what they've done to be more efficient or to do a better job. Sharing and learning helps create feelings of camaraderie that make for a more relaxing and enjoyable place to work.

- Avoid the pitfall of comparing yourself negatively to others. If someone else is achieving more than you are, rather than spend time putting yourself down, learn from that person. Compare yourself to yourself. Yes, you must be aware of what other people are accomplishing, but your efforts should be focused on creating and following your own vision and learning what you can from others along the way.

- Don't engage in talking negatively about your boss or your fellow employees. Understand that this is how many people build peer relationships at work, but simply refuse to participate. When someone bends your ear with a complaint, nod sympathetically, then change the subject, or remember something you need to do. You don't have to say a word, and people will quickly get the message that you're not game for that kind of thing. Not only will you raise the energy level in your workplace by refusing to participate, but you'll also set an excellent example for other coworkers who may not want to participate in office gossip either, but haven't yet figured out how to avoid it.

- Make a point of complimenting coworkers who've done a good job, even your competitors. If you're genuine in your praise, you'll help create a nurturing atmosphere in which it'll be easier for everyone to work. And you never know when your competitor might become your boss.

49. Zip Up

We know the human body is comprised of a matrix of subtle energies that we can naturally and consciously use to heal, empower, and balance ourselves. Thanks to the spread of the knowledge of many ancient energy healing systems, such as acupuncture, acupressure, qigong, tai chi, and numerous other forms of energy medicine, we're becoming more aware of how our physical energy systems work and how we can use our energy and these ancient techniques to heal and protect ourselves.

The simple truth is that until we learn to activate and safeguard our energy systems, someone else can easily interfere, consciously or unconsciously, with our energy and even influence or control how we feel. You've probably experienced this yourself. You can be feeling fantastic until you run into someone who says "Gee, you look awful. Are you okay?" All of a sudden your energy drops and you begin to feel terrible. What happens in this kind of situation is that the other person is feeling bad, so he projects how he feels onto you—and possibly onto other people he meets who are vulnerable. This is a perfect example of how someone else's energy can affect your own.

The body's central energy meridian governs the central nervous system. It runs like a zipper from your pubic bone up to your bottom lip, and is extremely sensitive to other people's energy. It acts like a radio receiver. It can pull someone else's energies directly into your energy system. One of the fastest and most powerful ways to take charge of your own energy and protect it from someone else's influence is to use the electromagnetic energies of your hands to trace, or "zip up," the central meridian.

You can use this ten-second technique whenever you're feeling vulnerable around other people and need to empower yourself, whenever you're meeting with people who drain your energy, or at any time you want to be at your optimum level of performance.

Here's how to zip up:

1. Take a deep breath—inhaling through your nose, exhaling through your mouth—while rubbing both hands together to activate the energy centers in your hands. (You may feel a sensation of warmth in your palms as you become more sensitive to this energy.)

2. Place your right palm several inches out from and facing your body at the level of your pubic bone (the bottom of the central meridian) and, while inhaling again, briskly bring your hand up to your lower lip, having the conscious intention of vitalizing your own energy while at the same time shielding your energy source from someone else's.

3. Repeat two or three times.

The central meridian energy naturally flows up the central channel. When you consciously trace the meridian in this manner, you strengthen the meridian and it strengthens you.

Try this right now and notice how it energizes you. The more you practice the zip up, the more centered and in control you'll feel. Get into the habit of using it any time you interact with others to help you connect with your own power and set the boundaries that you know are right for you.

50. Write It Before You Say It

Very often we do major damage to our work and personal relationships that can take years to mend by saying things to someone without thinking carefully beforehand.

The harm caused by the things we say—not to mention the stress and loss of productivity they produce—can be enormous. This hurt can create a wall in your workspace that can be difficult, if not impossible, to work through.

Here is a simple but powerful process you can use to eliminate that possibility in the future.

When you have something that is difficult to say to someone, or something that might be difficult for the person to hear, don't blurt it out. Rather, force yourself to follow a new approach.

First, think carefully about what you want to say. Then write it out so you can get a real feel for the impact your words might have.

Second, read it and say it aloud to yourself, so you can hear how it sounds. How often after a heated discussion with someone have you said to yourself, "How could I possibly have said *that?*" You're astounded at what came out of your mouth. If you listen ahead of time, you won't find yourself in that position.

Third, step into the other person's shoes. Be sensitive to the essential self of the other person, the part we each have that wants to do things right. Then hear yourself saying what you have to say. Notice how it feels. How would you react if you were the other person? Revise your statement as needed to be sure you're getting your message across without hurting the person or adding to the tension between you.

Finally, step back into your own shoes. Then say what you have to say.

It's imperative that you learn to set clear boundaries, but it's also important for you to value your work relationships enough to plan carefully before you speak your mind.

51. Breathe into It

Every time you interact with another person, either positively or negatively, you have an opportunity to access a whole multitude of growth-producing experiences. Our everyday work lives present endless possibilities for learning how to get along with all kinds of people in all kinds of situations. Approach your work life as a playing field where you can learn to excel in this vital skill.

Often, even with the best of intentions, you may find yourself embroiled in a conflict with a coworker that causes you to spend inordinate amounts of time feeling angry or frustrated. You may have attempted to work it out with the person, without success, or you may find yourself too intimidated to even try. This ongoing upset detracts from the quality and quantity of your work, and not being able to adequately resolve it adds to the stress.

What can you do in these situations? Learn to breathe into the problem with your full attention.

You can find a quiet spot where you won't be interrupted, or you can do this right at your desk or work area. You can keep your eyes open, or close them if you prefer. No one else has to know what you're doing.

Take a moment or two to feel where in your body the crux of this situation lies. Usually, if there is anger involved, we feel it in the solar plexus. You may feel a tightness or discomfort in your belly. Perhaps you feel a constriction in your chest or throat. You might notice you have a throbbing sensation in your temples. You may even have a headache, or a heartache, over this problem.

Once you've located the place in your body where you're holding this issue, keep your awareness there, then begin to breathe into that place. For example, if you feel it in your belly, be aware of what you're feeling there, and then breathe consciously slowly and deeply as if you were breathing into that sensation in your belly. Just stay with that sensation for a dozen breaths or so, and you'll notice some relief almost immediately.

There's wisdom in the breath. When you stay with the breathing for a few minutes, you'll not only be able to relieve the sensation and reduce the stress, but you'll also be able to develop clarity and insight. You don't have to try to figure anything out; let the understanding come to you.

Often the breathing relieves the anguish you're feeling, which makes it possible for you to get back to the work you were doing. Then, later, you may gain a fresh perspective that either makes it possible for you to let go of the anger completely or gives you a new vantage point from which to solve the problem. You may find yourself feeling compassion for the other person and understand why that person reacted the way he or she did. Or you may come to see how your own stubbornness created the problem to begin with. You'll recognize that you have so much more power and control when you interact with others from a place of understanding than when you're angry or upset.

Breathing into a problem—any problem—helps you to ease it, understand it, and solve it so much more quickly, and makes it possible for you to get back to the task at hand much more effectively.

FIVE

Being More Efficient with Your Money

52. Understand the Importance of Living Within Your Means

One of the biggest stumbling blocks for many people who want to simplify their work lives is their fear that if they cut back, they'll lose ground financially. If the financial considerations are a challenge for you, know that it's possible to build a secure financial base so you can simplify your work life. Often just by making one or two changes in the way you handle your finances, you'll be free to change the way you work.

After fifteen years in the real estate investment business, I became convinced that two financial issues keep people chained to long hours in work they don't like. The first is that most people have only a vague idea how much money they actually have to spend each month after taxes and other payroll deductions. Second, without that knowledge, it's difficult, if not impossible, to live within their means.

My beliefs were confirmed by two researchers, Drs. Thomas J. Stanley and William D. Danko, authors of *The Millionaire Next*

Door (Pocket Books, 1996). Their book outlines the findings of their twenty-year study of how people become millionaires. The authors point out that there's never been more personal wealth in America than there is today, yet nearly 97 percent of Americans, *including even most high-income earners*, are not wealthy. Why? Because, as this research shows, most Americans have developed a lifelong habit of spending more than they earn.

Unfortunately, our culture has operated on the belief that the appearance of wealth is more important than actual wealth. As a result, we have a nation of consumers up to their eyeballs in debt for products and services that make them look great but feel poor.

Here are some interesting facts from the Stanley and Danko research that help explain how only a very small percentage of Americans have become wealthy in these times of unprecedented wealth:

- The typical millionaires are not high-income earners. Many probably don't make much more than you do. They just spend less.
- The typical millionaires become financially secure by living on a budget and knowing exactly what they spend each month. They know that even high-income producers must live *below* their means if they intend to become financially independent.

- The typical millionaires have year in and year out set aside 20 percent or more of their after-tax income in a qualified retirement plan for the purpose of building a retirement nest egg. If the money they're allowed to set aside doesn't equal 20 percent of their after-tax income, they set up an additional retirement fund of their own to make up the difference, even though it may not be in a tax-deferred plan. Most often this money is invested in stocks and mutual funds with growth potential. These are people who've figured out that social security alone—or combined with the income Uncle Sam allows us to set aside tax deferred in a qualified retirement plan—most likely won't afford them a comfortable retirement.

- The typical millionaires have an average net worth of $1.6 million and are able to retire in their mid-fifties or earlier and live on the interest income from their retirement fund if they choose.

- Contrary to popular belief, 84 percent of today's millionaires earn their own wealth; they don't inherit it.

- The typical millionaires know they aren't the house they live in, the car they drive, or the clothes they wear. Therefore, they've become conscious consumers; they live in modest homes, drive modest cars, and never buy custom-made suits.

So the formula for acquiring true wealth is simple: Earn, save, and invest. Unfortunately, most Americans have it backward.

They earn and spend. And they have it doubly backward when they spend *more* than they earn. Spending more than they earn is the primary reason over 60 percent of Americans are struggling under moderate to heavy debt loads and why so many Americans aren't wealthy.

Most people have bought into the popular cultural conditioning that tells us we're not successful—we haven't achieved the American Dream—unless we live in a big house, drive the latest cars, wear the hottest fashions, and own all the other "necessities" credit card debt can buy. We're indoctrinated by television, magazines, movies, billboards, and advertising to believe not only that wealth equals worth but also that by *appearing* wealthy, we *are* wealthy.

But as many people are starting to figure out, just the opposite is true. As anyone who's done it knows, having to appear wealthy by going into debt is true poverty. It is poverty of truth. It is poverty of spirit.

One day you wake up and realize that struggling to appear successful by spending money you haven't earned doesn't make any sense. Falling deeper and deeper into debt just isn't worth it. The time has come to change our definition of success. What the Joneses think means considerably less when you realize that many of them aren't living within their means either.

The good news is that you can begin step by step to live by this wealth-building formula right now. Once you decide to do that, you'll begin to achieve control of your financial life. Having that control will open up a whole new world of work options that aren't available to you when you don't know where you stand financially.

In this part I outline a series of steps, one or more of which will help you gain control of your financial life. This isn't rocket science; it's very basic stuff. But these are concepts most people are never taught, so they may seem foreign at first. If you understand the principles involved and put them into practice, you'll be able to live within your means. This is the first step toward building the financial security that will make it easier to simplify your work life.

53. Figure Out Your Monthly After-Tax Income

Jennifer, the daughter of a friend of mine, graduated from college a few years ago and had what seemed at the time the good fortune to land a salaried position in the film industry that paid $39,000 a year. She was thrilled to be starting at a level that was beyond what she'd anticipated for a first job. She'd been used to summer jobs that paid $6.00 to $8.00 an hour, and now, she calculated, she was earning $3,250 per month, or $750 per week, or roughly $18.75 an hour ($39,000 divided by 52 weeks = $750 per week, divided by 40 hours = $18.75 an hour)

Knowing she was going to be earning such a handsome salary, before she started work she rented a modest studio apartment and, with two newly acquired credit cards, went on a shopping spree to decorate it. In addition to buying a new bed, a desk, chairs, and lamps, she purchased the basic "necessities," including a television, a CD player, a cappuccino maker, linens, and other items she thought she'd need. She has a generous nature, and because she now felt flush after five penurious years as a student, she increased her credit card debt even more by spending lavishly on gifts for her two siblings and her mother. She knew she had college loans to pay back, but she had a year before she had to start worrying about that.

Jennifer started out, as many of us have, working more hours than the standard forty-hour workweek on which her salary had been based. She wanted to set off on the right foot, learn as much as she could about this fascinating new career, and let her bosses know that she was willing to go the extra mile. Little by little her weekly hours increased. By the end of the first six months she was working fifty-five to sixty hours a week. By the end of the first year she was putting in close to seventy hours a week, working both evenings and weekends. Since she was a salaried employee her employer was not required to pay her for any time she worked beyond forty hours a week.

In addition to the time she actually spent in the office, Jennifer gradually found she was on call to her bosses pretty much around the clock. It wasn't unusual for her to arrive home at 10 P.M., exhausted and ready to fall into bed (the very one she was still paying off on her credit card), only to get an urgent call asking her to come back to the office to wrap up a report that had to be ready first thing the next morning. She didn't mind so much. After all, her bosses seemed impressed with her abilities and were lavish in their praise of her talents. They as much as promised her a piece of her own development deal some day.

During that first year she barely had time to take care of the cleaning, shopping, laundry, and basic maintenance needs, so she certainly didn't have the time to stop and figure out that the standard payroll deductions for federal, state, city, and social security taxes reduced her income by roughly 30 percent. This meant that while nominally she was earning $18.75 an hour, her after-tax wage had dropped to $13.12 an hour. Here's where the problem starts. This $5.63 per hour difference doesn't sound like a lot, but it adds up quickly. It meant that Jennifer had nearly a thousand dollars less each month to live on than she'd thought.

Jennifer woke up one morning a year and a half after she had taken the job and realized that she had more than $10,000 in credit card debt, and she'd only just begun paying down the college loan debt. She was exhausted and burned out. She wanted desperately to quit her job, but she was so deep in debt she didn't see how she could possibly do so. And she had no idea how any of this had happened.

Five years have passed. Jennifer just recently paid off the credit card debt, after cutting up her credit cards and going on a spending diet. She got help from an uncle in paying down some of her college loans but still has a way to go with them. She stayed with the film industry job for a total of two years before she got up the nerve to quit and find a job that gave her back her life.

I encourage you to take the time right now, if you haven't already done so, to figure out your true monthly income after taxes and other payroll deductions. This is the starting figure you'll need to know in order to begin living within your means.

In addition you might also find it helpful to calculate your true after-tax *hourly* wage.

Jennifer eventually figured out that, based on the fact that she was actually working seventy hours a week, her *hourly* rate had changed, too. It had dropped—nearly one-half—to $10.71 an hour ($750 a week before taxes divided by 70 hours = $10.71 per hour).

But, even worse, *after* taxes her seventy-hour workweek, reduced her hourly rate to $7.50 an hour ($525 a week after taxes divided by 70 hours).

Even if you're a salaried employee, take the time to figure out your true hourly wage. It'll be illuminating for you to know how much you're earning *per hour* after taxes. With that figure it'll be easy to calculate your after-tax hourly income based on the number of hours you actually work, rather than based on your nominal forty-hour week. This number will give you a better idea of the amount by which your hourly wage is reduced by each additional hour you spend working. If you're on the road to becoming financially secure, you'll want to know what working those extra hours contributes to your bottom line.

54. Understand the Law of
Diminishing Returns

In telling Jennifer's story I'm not suggesting that one should never work long hours. If Jennifer had truly loved what she was doing, and if there'd been even a reasonable chance she could get ahead doing it, it might have been worth it for her to jump in with both feet and take whatever time it took to succeed. But there are two important things to consider when doing that.

The first is to know what the odds are of actually getting ahead in the industry or in the job in which you're working. Jennifer learned later that her bosses had run through half a dozen young would-be filmmakers before she came along. Each had been promised the moon and had been worked to a frazzle. Jennifer outlasted them all, even her two successors, who both caught on faster than she did and departed quickly.

It's possible to point to many industries today, most notoriously the computer industry, where this is often the case. Yes, if you strike it rich with a company that goes public, you can end up very wealthy. But if you're going to ransom your heart and soul and your body, mind, and spirit—not to mention your family—to get ahead, you'll want to have a clear perception of what the odds are that those long hours will contribute to your success, financial and otherwise. In Jennifer's case, the odds of moving ahead in that position were close to zero.

Second, while working long hours may give you an advantage in the beginning, you very quickly reach a point of diminishing returns. The long hours I put in early in my investment career were beneficial. I entered the investment world with a background in English literature. I knew I had to work overtime just to learn the basics of finance and to develop an understanding of how the numbers worked. For the first year or so, those long hours probably helped me.

But I see now that, after a certain point, I didn't actually need to put in ten hours a day; it was simply habit. Ultimately all that overtime contributed little if anything to my success and added little if anything to my bottom line. In fact, beyond that first year or two, many of the extra hours I put in over the course of fifteen years were counterproductive. The extra time was exhausting, created considerable stress, and eventually led to burnout. Had I taken the time to create more balance in my life as I went along, I'd have been able to bring much more clarity, creativity, and intuitive understanding to my investment career, and I'd have avoided the less than rewarding investment decisions I made.

It's ironic that after a certain point, much of the overtime I put into my career turned out to be a poor investment. While this is not always the case, it happens more than you might want to believe. I encourage you to take the time to carefully analyze what you truly gain—financially, emotionally, spiritually—by working a grueling workweek.

55. Develop a Basic Understanding of the Tax Laws

Now that you know your monthly after-tax income, keep in mind that many factors can change that figure from year to year. Your after-tax income can be changed, either positively or negatively, by any of the following:

Marriage

Divorce

An increase or decrease in the number of dependents you have

Social security or self-employment taxes

The purchase or sale of your home

A job change

A change in your spouse's income

Medical expenses

Travel expenses

Home office use

Mortgage interest

Investment gains and losses

Itemized deductions you claim

Interest and dividend income

Capital gains and losses

Casualty losses

Insurance reimbursements

Supplemental income

Depreciation and amortization

And the sale of business property, among others

The financially secure person has taken the time to build a firm understanding of how these and other factors will affect his or her monthly income. If you want to build financial security, you'll want to take the time to develop a firm understanding, too. This is not difficult; it just takes time.

As we saw in Parts 1 and 2, when you start cutting back on

the number of hours you work each week, you'll free up a considerable amount of time. If you don't already have a handle on your financial picture, it would make sense for you to spend some of that time getting a handle on it. Consider the absurdity of working fifty or sixty or more hours each week to make more money, only to fall behind financially because you haven't taken the time to figure out what you have to do to keep the money you make.

This doesn't mean you have to completely understand the intricacies of the tax laws. No one, not even God Herself, completely understands them. But it does mean you must have a basic grasp of how your monthly income is affected by many of the things you do. Set aside time each week for several months to get up to speed on your tax picture. Here are some things you can do:

- Read several of the most up-to-date books on how to save on taxes, then set up a plan to implement the tax-savings techniques that are applicable to your situation. Even if you're presently unable to lower your tax liability significantly, reading these books will give you a basic understanding of how taxes affect your bottom line. Two tax books I recommend are *Cut Your Taxes* by Kevin McCormally (Kiplinger Books, 1998) and *Year-Round Tax Strategies* by J. K. Lasser (IDG Books, 1999).

- Take a tax class through your local adult education program. Talk to the class instructor and other knowledgeable people so you can begin to get a grasp of how the tax numbers work.

- Once you have a basic understanding of taxes, invest $50 in a tax software program and learn to work the numbers to see how various financial decisions you might make or have made affect your net after-tax income.

- Next, pay your tax preparer for a couple of hours of his or her time to review your past several tax returns. After following the above suggestions, you'll have a better idea of the right questions to ask relative to your circumstances. Make sure you have a tax preparer who speaks English (as opposed to one who speaks "Accountant") and who doesn't talk down to you. Never make a significant investment move without checking with your tax advisor first. Do this not only to avoid doing something that would negatively affect your net after-tax income, but so you truly understand the tax consequences and you're not caught unaware at tax filing time.

Taxes can eat up 20 percent to 30 percent or more of your earnings each year. Not only is it vital for you to understand how that tax bite reduces your monthly income, but you must understand that practically every move you make can affect, either positively or negatively, the amount you keep after taxes.

It's my personal belief that the tax laws in this country are so grotesquely complicated and out of line because the majority of income earners have been too busy earning a living to take the time to figure out how much of it they forfeit each year to taxes. If every single taxpayer in America took the steps I've outlined here, and finally began to understand what's happening to their income after taxes, you can bet there'd be a tax revolution and a simpler tax code.

56. Appreciate the Time Value of Money

In the next item I'll talk about the importance of paying yourself first. But before we get there, I want you to understand why paying yourself first is so critical to your financial success and ultimately to your ability to keep your work life in balance. If you don't get this concept, its unlikely you'll see the importance of paying yourself first, getting started early if you haven't already done so, and keeping your money invested for the long haul.

Einstein believed the most important concept of the twentieth century for the average person was the time value of money. There are various components to this concept, but for our purposes the most important is that when money is invested, and the return on that money is reinvested, it grows exponentially, as in 1, 2, 4, 8, 16, 32, and so forth. So money doubles on itself over time.

To determine how much time it'll take for a certain amount of money to double at a certain rate of return, you can use the rule of 72, in which you divide the rate of return into 72. The rule of 72 is an approximation, but if you invest $5,000 at 10 percent, it will double in 7.2 years (72 divided by 10 equals 7.2). If you invest $5,000 at 8 percent, it will double in 9 years (72 divided by 8 equals 9), and so forth.

So, for example, if you invest $5,000 at 10 percent, it will be worth approximately $10,000 in 7.2 years.

In another 7.2 years it will be worth $20,000.

In another 7.2 years it will be worth $40,000.

In another 7.2 years it will be worth $80,000.

In another 7.2 years it will be worth $160,000.

And in another 7.2 years, or a total of 43.2 years (roughly an average working life), it will be worth approximately $300,000.

If you don't understand that money doubles exponentially, you can very easily lose patience. You might think, "I'm never going to get ahead," and spend the $10,000 after seven years or less. It seems like such a small amount and that it will never make a difference to your retirement income. This is what happens with most people. And as we know, in this culture there are so many temptations to spend that money.

But it makes a *huge* difference. If you see that in the later years a substantial sum is doubling on top of itself, you'll develop the discipline to pay yourself first, month in and month out, and develop the patience to delay your present spending for future growth. This is why it's so important to live within your means, especially during your early income-earning years. The money you set aside when you're young will have a longer period of time in which to grow exponentially.

For example, a person earning the median income of $38,174 at age thirty would need to set aside roughly 11 percent of his income, or $4,199 per year through his working years, to achieve a reasonable level of financial security at the retirement age of sixty-five to sustain his standard of living (inflation adjusted) to age eighty-five. A forty-year-old earning the median income of $46,359 would need to set aside 22 percent of his annual income, or $10,199 per year. A fifty-year-old earning the median income of $51,875 would need to set aside 51 percent of his annual income, or $26,456 per year.

The variables in savings are *time*, the *amount* saved, and the *rate of return*. If you start when you're young, you don't have to save a lot, you just have to be systematic and disciplined. Without discipline you're nowhere. As you can see from the above example, you can replace time with either a higher percentage of savings or higher rates of return (which means much higher risk), but saving a higher amount later is more difficult and much more painful than saving less at lower risk.

Once you see how your money grows when you add to it each month by paying yourself first, and how it grows exponentially over the years until you retire, you won't wait to build up to that 20 percent minimum that the typical millionaire sets aside each month; you'll start right now.

57. Pay Yourself First

Remember, one of the first steps in building financial security is figuring out how much money you actually have to live on each month after taxes and other payroll deductions. But if you want to be in control of your present and future financial life, there are several other calculations you need to make before you know the actual means within which you'll plan to live.

The first calculation is to figure out the amount you'll need to deduct from your after-tax income each month for long-term wealth building. This is the money you will pay yourself that will go into a qualified retirement plan. Many people believe that contributing the maximum amount they're allowed under the tax law to a qualified retirement plan is sufficient, especially if their employer is matching their contribution. Though sometimes that amount is sufficient to generate a comfortable retirement nest egg, more often it is not. Make sure you know what percentage of your after-tax income you're able to set aside in your qualified retirement plan, and then decide how much more you'll need to set aside to meet your future retirement needs.

Keep in mind that the typical millionaire pays himself first by setting aside up to 20 percent of his after-tax income, and many set aside an even higher percentage. Twenty percent is a conservative amount and is easily doable if you understand the time value of money and establish the discipline to pay yourself first.

If you're not currently setting aside money for a retirement fund, or if you know the money going into your qualified plan won't be sufficient to build your retirement nest egg, arrange now to pay yourself first. To begin with, set aside at least 5 percent of your net after-tax income each month. Then set up a simple investment plan (#63) and put this money to work for your future. As you get your expenses under control (#62), you can increase that percentage month by month and year by year until the amount you set aside for retirement is at least 20 percent of your net after-tax income.

Don't underestimate the importance of paying yourself first. Millions of people have made the mistake of thinking they'll start next year, or when their kids are older, or at any time other than now. But unless you're planning to inherit a couple million dollars from a rich aunt, starting now could make a big difference in ensuring you a comfortable retirement income versus one that will barely support you or may not support you at all. The sooner you get started, the more money you'll build into your retirement fund. And once you get started, the easier it'll be to continue.

Before you start paying yourself first, make certain that you've paid off all your credit card debt. It doesn't make sense to pay 18 percent interest on your consumer debt while you're earning only 10 percent interest as an annual average on your investment portfolio.

Many advisors suggest that before you start investing in a retirement fund, you set money aside for contingencies, which I'll talk about next, *before* you start investing in a retirement fund. But I heartily disagree. You need to get started immediately, if not sooner, putting money into your retirement fund. When you defer qualified plan contributions, you not only lose the time value of money, you irrevocably lose tax benefits. The benefits of having funds growing tax deferred are considerable. For example, if you invested $1,000 for forty years at 10 percent a year and paid taxes on the investment income each year at 33 percent, it would grow to $13,384. But, it would more than double to $30,323 if annual taxes were deferred in a qualified retirement plan and then paid at the end of the forty years on the entire accumulated investment income.

58. Build a Contingency Fund and a College Education Fund

Since that 20 percent you'll soon be deducting from your after-tax income is retirement money that is not to be used for anything but building long-term financial security, the next step is to set aside money for a contingency savings fund.

This fund will ensure that it won't be necessary for you to dig into your retirement funds when the water heater breaks or you're faced with uncovered medical expenses, or have to fly to Omaha to help an ailing parent through an emergency. The percentage of after-tax income you should set aside for contingencies will vary depending on your age, whether you rent or own your own home, the age of your home and the condition it's in, as well as other personal circumstances.

One way to help you determine an appropriate amount is to go back through your personal and household maintenance expenses for the past several years to come up with the average annual expenditures. (Use your check register and your credit card statements to do this if you don't yet have a budget established.) You want to avoid getting caught short for these "unexpected" expenses, which may tempt you to raid your retirement fund or put you in the position of having to borrow money. Doing so will only create more debt and more stress, and contribute to that helpless feeling of being out of control with your finances.

To begin with, a reasonable minimum figure to set aside each month for a personal and household contingency fund might be 5 percent of your after-tax income. And since this contingency fund is constantly being depleted by these "unexpected" expenses, you'll want to continue setting aside anywhere from 3 to 5 percent or more of your after-tax income each month year in and year out. This percentage can easily be adjusted up or down several years down the road when you have a better idea what your expenses in these areas actually are.

Eventually your contingency fund should be sufficient to cover your living expenses for three to six months or more. In fact, many advisors suggest that you have enough money set aside to support you and your family for at least a year, ideally two years. Your contingency funds should be invested in liquid assets such as bank savings accounts or, preferably, money market mutual funds.

Also, if you have kids and plan to help put them through college, you may also want to have a separate college investment fund for each child. With the rapid changes occurring with on-line education, our ideas about a college education could soon be radically different from what they are today. But it's likely that traditional avenues of learning will be viable for the fore-seeable future.

At the present time, a four-year college education can cost anywhere from $50,000 to $100,000. Over the next ten to fifteen years, these figures could conceivably double. Obviously, the amount a family sets aside for college varies greatly, depending on their circumstances, their children's interests, and other factors.

You can use a computerized program such as Quicken to help you determine how much you'll need to set aside and how much you can accumulate by the time your kids reach college age. You can also go online to scholarshare.com, collegesav-ings.org or savingforcollege.com to find other sources of tuition income for your kids. Scholarshare.com helps you calculate how much money you'll need, based on your children's current ages, and offers programs that will help you put away money that can grow tax deferred, then be taxed at your child's tax rate when it's withdrawn. Savingforcollege.com will help you figure out how to utilize one of the tax-advantaged 529 plans.

Now of course you might say, "To heck with that. Let the kids put themselves through college." And many people do that, either by choice or by necessity. But typical millionaires spend heavily for their children's education, and if they can do it, so can you. Remember, the typical millionaire doesn't make all that much more than you do; in fact, many probably make less. But, because they're more concerned with having wealth than with the appearance of wealth, they live on a far smaller percentage of their gross income than nonmillionaires do. A large portion of the 97 percent of the American population who are not millionaires could be millionaires if they made different choices—if they chose to spend less and to live within their means and invest the difference.

Having money set aside in these contingency funds will greatly expand your options should you decide to take some time off to explore other work possibilities or to take a cut in pay to begin a new career that enables you to have balance in your life.

If you haven't already done so, I strongly urge you to take the time to calculate your after-tax income. Then deduct the monthly contributions you'll need to make to your retirement fund, your contingency funds, and your kids' college savings funds. This will give you your means—the net dollars you actually have to live on each month. You may be in better shape than you thought, but if you aren't, knowing where you are will make it possible for you to figure out what you need to do to get where you want to be.

59. Know How Much House You Can Afford

If you've gone through the previous exercises with your income figures, you'll now have a much clearer idea about your true financial picture. This will help you determine what you can truly and comfortably afford to pay for your home. The chances are great that the amount you can afford is considerably less than the amount most mortgage lenders would approve.

The biggest expense by far for the average family is housing. In the past thirty years, the size of the typical American home has nearly tripled from an average of 900 square feet to 2,200 square feet. In many parts of the country, the cost of the now-typical three-bedroom, two-bath house has increased nearly sevenfold during that time.

Conventional financial planning wisdom for the last fifty years has said that you should spend no more than 25 percent of your gross monthly income for your total housing cost, including principal, interest, taxes, and insurance (PITI). That is still sound advice.

Unfortunately, lenders have increased that percentage considerably in recent years, often with drastic consequences for the borrower. Today many lenders around the country approve loans based on a ratio of roughly 39 percent of gross monthly income (assuming there's no other debt) for a down payment of 10 percent or less and, unbelievably, up to 49 percent for a 20 percent down payment.

Looking at the after-tax, after–retirement fund, after–contingency fund, and after–college fund numbers from the previous exercises, you can see that someone paying 39 percent to 49 percent of their gross income for a mortgage payment wouldn't have a lot left each month to live on.

For example, someone in a 30 percent tax bracket earning a $40,000 median income would have roughly $2,333 as a monthly after-tax income on which to live ($40,000 × 30 percent tax rate = $12,000 in taxes, which leaves an annual income of $28,000, divided by 12 months = $2,333 a month, after taxes).

If he spent 39 percent of his $3,333 *gross* income, or $1,299, on a monthly PITI payment, this would leave only $1,034 a month to cover all other expenses ($2,333 − $1,299 = $1,034).

If from the $1,034 amount he deducted even only 5 percent of his after-tax income, or $116 a month ($2,333 × .05), for his retirement investment fund, this would leave $918 as a net (after tax) net (after investments) monthly income.

He wouldn't be able to put the full 20 percent that the typical financially secure individual sets aside, or $466 of his after-tax income, into a retirement fund, since he'd then have only $452 per month to cover all his other expenses, and this isn't counting deductions for his contingency and college funds.

Lenders do a tremendous disservice to the home-buying public by approving loans that are far more than what buyers can actually afford. Loan officers will tell you they've increased the percentages because the cost of housing has risen so dramatically. Thus if they didn't approve loans whose payments are up to 40 to 50 percent of the gross income, borrowers wouldn't qualify for the loan and couldn't then buy the homes they want. Lenders say they just want to make it possible for home buyers to do that.

But don't you believe it. Lenders don't make loans for the benefit of the buyer; they make loans for their own benefit. That's how they make their money. When it comes to their bottom line, their primary concern is whether you'll continue to make the monthly payment. It's of no consequence to the lender if it puts you under tremendous emotional, financial, and work pressure to do so.

Yes, in the short term, approving the loan puts home buyers into the "home of their dreams," a home that is in many cases considerably beyond what they can actually afford. But in the long run such high loan payments keep borrowers struggling to make the payments, often prevent them from building long-term wealth other than their increased housing equity, keep them shackled to unsatisfying jobs, and add incredible stress to their lives.

Obviously there are many circumstances to take into consideration when you're buying a home. You may choose to pay more for a home in a neighborhood with an outstanding or uniquely focused school your child would like to attend. If you're buying into an area with rapidly appreciating housing prices, the increase in equity after a few years might make it worthwhile for you to stretch for a mortgage payment that would eventually make it possible for you to take advantage of the corresponding increase in your equity that the appreciation provides. The location in relation to your place of work, ailing parents, commuter transportation, medical services, and ease of basic shopping needs might all be other factors you need to consider.

But in calculating how much you can reasonably afford to pay for your monthly housing expense, keep in mind one sure thing: The typical millionaires have learned that it's vastly easier to live within their means in less expensive homes in simple neighborhoods, surrounded by other people with simple wants and needs, than it is to allow a lender to determine how much they can afford to pay on their mortgages.

60. Consider Moving to a Smaller Home

As we've just seen, home buyers frequently get approved for loans that are far larger than they can actually afford, then struggle mightily to keep up with the payments. If they can hold on and can keep making the mortgage payments, increases in their income might make the payments more manageable after a few years. But in the meantime, at least two things happen.

First, they've not been able to set aside any money for retirement wealth building or for emergencies. If the furnace has to be replaced and they have no contingency funds available, they often have to borrow more, either through bank loans or credit cards. That added debt becomes another burden that keeps them chained to an unhappy job situation and adds to the stress in their lives.

Second, the longer people wait to begin the habit of setting aside funds for wealth building, the harder it is to ever get started. And then once they do get started, they have to set aside an even higher percentage of their income than they would if they'd started earlier. While it's true that home ownership is an important part of wealth building, you want to make sure the amount you pay for that ownership is reasonably within your means.

Third, many families are living in homes that are far larger than they actually need and require that both parents work full time in order to meet the payments. Many times moving to a smaller home would make it possible for one parent to devote more time to the kids while the family could still live within their means.

Fourth, having bought a house that is more than they can afford, the average couple then goes on to spend more than they can afford outfitting the house and themselves and their kids so they can live up to the neighborhood image of "success." Having to continue to live up to that image is one of the biggest factors that adds to the complexity of our work lives today.

Many of the people who're making changes in their lives and are cutting back are doing so because it's finally dawned on them that they're paying far more for their homes than they can afford. Yes, they may be able to meet that mortgage payment each month, but after doing so they have little or nothing left to put into their retirement funds, and they're constantly stressed by money issues. These are people who're realizing that by living more simply they can work more simply. These are people who've figured out that those who love and value them will love and value them no matter what house they live in.

Home ownership is a vital part of a long-term wealth-building program. If you buy the right house in the right area at the right time, the increase in equity can add significantly to your net worth over the long haul, and the tax savings of home ownership can enhance your wealth-building fund if you invest them accordingly. But there's a big difference between stretching a bit beyond your current ability to buy a house you'll soon be able to comfortably afford and buying well beyond your true means and in the process greatly complicating and even endangering your financial life over the long haul. I urge you to analyze your monthly mortgage payments carefully to make sure you're not being forced by your monthly housing expense to spend your retirement money before you've had a chance to invest it.

If you find that what you're paying for your home makes it impossible to set aside money for your future, I encourage you to take whatever steps are necessary to keep your monthly housing payment within your means, even if it means moving to a less expensive home.

I realize that having to consider the prospect of moving

"down" might be a challenging thought for you. The fear of what one's neighbors or family or friends might think often keeps us living beyond our means. But having done it myself, and after hearing regularly from readers who've taken similar steps, I can assure you that the confidence and power you'll gain from being in control of your financial life will far outweigh any concerns you may have about what someone else thinks. Consider the insanity of allowing your financial decisions to be based on the opinions of someone whose regard for you is ruled by the number of square feet you occupy.

Getting your financial life under control will open the doorway to the possibility of financial growth that you can't even envision when you're weighed down by the strain of living beyond your means. It's almost impossible to let your creative instincts soar when your psyche is stifled by debt.

61. Avoid Consumer Debt and Debt Consolidation

According to recent financial reports, household debt has exceeded after-tax income for the first time in history. This means, for example, that someone earning an annual after-tax income of $50,000 can owe $50,000 a year or more on combined housing, credit card, and other consumer debt. This is a situation you don't want to be in; if you understand the basics of this chapter, and live by them, you never will.

When the financial burden of spending more than they earn becomes too great, borrowers often fall for loan consolidation schemes that, in my opinion, are the black holes of personal finance. Unscrupulous lenders entice people to refinance their home loans, sometimes for as much as 150 percent of the home's value, by rolling all their consumer debt—for cars, vacations, and other consumer purchases—into a new home loan.

Consider the insanity of this. With a reconsolidation home loan, borrowers will now be paying off debt on a car, for example, for thirty years even though three, five, or ten years from now they may no longer own the car. Even if they do still own it, it'll be worth only a small fraction of what they paid for it, and they'll be paying interest on the original purchase price for thirty years! Or, worse, they'll be paying interest on credit card debt they incurred for miscellaneous gewgaws they don't remember buying. Or worse yet, by using their home equity to pay for these gewgaws, they lose one of the primary benefits of home owner-ship, equity appreciation.

Consider the plight of a couple I know who, in their early fifties, was convinced by their banker to refinance their home loan. They had only ten years left to pay on their mortgage, which was set at a reasonable fixed rate that they could handle comfortably. But they'd incurred close to $20,000 debt in re-modeling expenses and other miscellaneous credit card expen-ditures, and they wanted to get out from under that debt. After refinancing they were paying off the combined debt (the amount of the original loan balance and the remodeling and other debt) at an initially lower variable interest rate than they were paying previously.

This lower rate was what attracted them to the idea of re-financing. But this rate will rise as the Fed increases interest rates; so potentially they soon could have to make monthly payments considerably higher than their old fixed rate. Most frightening of all, they'll be making payments on this loan until they're eighty years old.

Though they didn't want to believe it, this couple was never in the position to spend money they didn't have on remodeling, and they'd let their credit card spending get out of control.

With a consolidation loan, borrowers extend the number of years they have to pay off the debt, thereby paying significantly more in interest payments over the long term. But even worse, these schemes give borrowers the feeling that their financial lives are finally under control. With this false sense of security, they can easily fall back into their out-of-control spending habits and go into debt all over again. People in these situations often end up paying interest on their interest payments and seldom get even, let alone get ahead.

This is exactly where credit card companies want you to be. Jennifer (#53) actually believed that the credit card companies were so nice not to insist that she pay off the full amount she'd charged each month. She simply didn't understand, as many people don't, that she was paying through the nose for that "privilege."

You'll also want to avoid transferring your balances to a new credit card that offers a low come-on rate. Many of these teaser rates don't apply to older debt. Unless you're disciplined enough to pay the lower rate debt off completely while at the same time not adding to your debt, changing credit cards every few months to catch a lower rate is a losing game.

A far better plan for paying down debt would be to establish a realistic budget and become a conscious consumer (#62). Then put the money you're saving on your spending diet toward paying off your credit card and other consumer debt. Doing this could take several years, depending on the amount you owe and how much you can pay toward debt reduction each month. But tightening your belt and taking even four or five years to get out of debt is preferable to extending your debt out into the future for thirty years with a debt-consolidation loan.

If your credit card debt is overwhelming you, take some drastic measures. Eliminate all but one or two of your cards, which you'll use for emergencies only. A pocketful of credit cards is an invitation to spend money you don't have on things you don't need. Don't charge anything on your credit card that you can't pay in full by the end of the month. If you do this, the rate a credit card company charges on the unpaid balance is irrelevant since you won't have a balance. Remember that with the exception of his or her home, the typical millionaire avoids debt, and never buys anything that he or she can't pay for in full by the end of the month.

If you feel you are completely out of control in terms of your debt, read *The Unofficial Guide to Beating Debt* by Greg Pahl (IDG Books, 2000). Keep in mind that steep credit card debt is hazardous to your health. Recent research has shown that those with a high ratio of credit card debt not only feel more stress, they report more general health problems.

Financially secure people use a credit card as a convenience to limit the amount of cash they have to carry around; they never treat it as a portable debt-building device. Anyone who's striving for financial independence should adopt that policy as well.

62. Become a Conscious Consumer

If you're feeling that your financial life is out of control, closely examine your spending habits. You'll see that the antidote to excessive consumer debt is not to work more; rather it is to spend less.

Remember that the typical millionaire has learned to live within a budget. If you haven't been paying attention to your spending, begin now to do so. There are dozens of good books that will help you set up a budget. Find one that works for you, set up a spending plan, and stick with it.

This isn't to say it'll be easy. Living within your means may require you to take a whole new approach to the way you've been spending money. You may have to go without many things you think you want. You may have to let go of what other people think. You'll have to replace instant gratification with self-discipline and long-term planning. Perhaps most challenging of all, you may have to help your spouse and kids understand the importance of living within your means.

Here are some steps you can take to help you become more conscious about your consumer spending habits.

- Establish a new policy for the things you and your family members buy. Make the commitment that if you come across something you feel you absolutely must have, you'll put it on a list and post it on the family bulletin board for 30 days. Chances are good that by the end of the month, the impulse to have it will be gone. If it isn't, put the item back on the list for another thirty days. If you decide you want it, you can practically guarantee that it'll still be there waiting for you, possibly on sale. If it isn't available, you'll see that you'll survive well without it. This enforced policing of your buying patterns will help you see how often you acquire stuff without being conscious of how it affects your bottom line, not to mention the clutter in your life.

- Become familiar with your buying patterns by setting aside a reverse-spending month. For thirty days, don't buy anything but food and absolute necessities, then evaluate the experience and ask yourself some questions. Was it difficult to resist the urge to make impulse purchases? Do you truly miss not having the things you didn't buy? How much money did you save? How would your life be different if you lived this way all the time?

- Before you begin your reverse-spending plan, come up with your own definition of "absolute necessities." For example, if you use your car to commute to work, it might be necessary for you to replace the tires when they wear out, but it wouldn't be necessary to replace the tape deck if it broke. If the fridge conks out, you'll need to get another one, but if the TV dies, bury it and don't get a new one. (Watch the Lakers games with friends on their TV.)

- Get into the habit of looking at your true hourly wage—after taxes and divided by the number of hours you actually work (#53)—in order to determine how many extra hours you must work to buy something you're considering buying. You'll begin to see the absurdity of much of what you bring into your life. ("I'm working sixty hours to buy *that*?")
- Here are some other things you can do:

Train yourself to never go shopping without a list.

Don't buy anything unless it's on your list.

Don't window shop.

Stay out of the mall.

Take your name off mail-order catalog lists.

Designate one day a week as shopping day and stay out of stores and shopping centers except on your shopping day.

Shop alone. You'll save money and time. Studies have shown that women spend twice the time when they shop with their spouses or kids, and they also spend 20 percent more. They spend 30 percent more when they shop with friends.

Never grocery shop when you're hungry; you'll spend more money.

Arrange your shopping so you never have to shop when you're tired and your defenses against clever sales enticements are weakest.

Use a bank card instead of a credit card. It provides the same convenience, but you'll constantly be aware that the money you're spending is gone. It'll change the way you buy.

Getting your spending habits under control can be challenging, but it'll also be one of the most liberating things you'll ever do. It will pave the way for eventual financial independence and will make it possible for you to choose a job that nourishes your soul rather than being forced to take a job whose sole purpose is to help you pay off monthly debts or consume more.

63. Set Up a Simple Investment Plan

The most important step in becoming financially secure is to figure out what your true means are and learn to live within them. The second most important step is to consistently pay yourself first out of those means and to set up a simple investment plan so those payments can be made to work for you.

So another important way to spend some of your newfound time, if you haven't done so already, is to figure out how to best invest the money you're setting aside for retirement. You may have an excellent investment plan available to you through your employer. But if not, or if you have additional funds set aside in a nonqualified retirement plan, I urge you to read, study, and talk to people who know about investments that are suitable to your age, temperament, investment time line, and financial and personal circumstances.

If you're considering stock investments, one of the best approaches I've come across is *Common Sense on Mutual Funds—*

New Imperatives for the Intelligent Investor, by John C. Bogle (Wiley, 1999). John Bogle is the founder and senior chairman of The Vanguard Group, the world's largest no-load mutual fund group, with more than 10 million shareholders and $400 billion in assets. His straightforward, practical book outlines a simple, cost-effective, tax-advantaged plan of investing in index funds. Many financial advisors believe index funds are the wave of the future, especially for the long term investor.

This book and Bogle's strategy have been applauded by some of the best investment minds of the past fifty years. Invest $25 in this book, then invest time over the next few months reading it, reading it again, understanding it, working the numbers, and reading it again. This is a thick, dense book, packed with a wealth of wisdom about how to invest. It's not a quick read. It's not a get-rich-quick approach. But taking the time to read it might well be one of the best investments of time and money you'll ever make.

Don't be distracted by all the talk about the new economy. As Bogle points out, there have been numerous "new economies" in the past hundred years, but none has lasted. As he says, "Let the brief and uncertain years roll by, and face the future with faith. Perhaps a future winter will be longer and colder than usual, or a summer will be drier and hotter. In the long run, however, our economy and our financial markets are stable and rational. Don't let short-run fluctuations, market psychology, false hope, fear, and greed get in the way of good investment judgment."

Many financial planners and stock brokers want you to believe that investing is complicated so you'll pay them for their expertise. But as Bogle will show you, wise investing is quite simple, and to earn the highest returns that are realistically possible, you should invest with simplicity. His book will show you step by step exactly how to do that.

Once you've worked out your own simple investing plan, either on your own or with John Bogle's help, consult a financial planner if it'll make you feel more comfortable. If you don't already have one, find a reputable financial planner who charges by the hour rather than by commission. Never pay a financial advisor who would put you into investments on which he or she will earn a commission. No one can advise you objectively when he earns separate commissions from the investments he recommends to you.

When you find someone you like and trust, check with him or her several times a year to make sure your investment plan is still on track. Before you add to your simple portfolio or consider making a change, call your advisor to get his or her opinion. And go back and read John Bogle's book every year or so.

Never let someone else manage your money for you. The typical millionaires take the time to figure out how to manage their own money. You should plan to do that, too. Keep your own portfolio in your own name, make your own investment decisions with the input of a financial planner you know and trust, and never, ever give someone else the power over a discretionary account. If you don't now have time to make your own investment decisions, you're too busy. Figure out what you can let go of so you can keep your finger on the pulse of your own investments. (If you're invested in mutual funds, which are one of the few investments that makes long-term sense for the average investor, they're run by managers. These are the only managers you need.)

Don't make the mistake of believing that investing has gotten too complicated and that you need to have someone else manage your account for you. Maintaining an investment plan, like anything else, is easy once you know how.

Never rush into a financial plan or allow someone else to rush you. With a wealth-building portfolio you're not worried about market timing; you're investing for the long haul. Take a reasonable amount of time to make sure the plan you're considering is suitable for you. Any lost opportunity in the short term will be more than offset by the benefits of a long-term strategy.

The Schwab Center for Investment Research recently updated a classic study on market timing, conducted over the past twenty years. The study revealed that if you'd invested $2,000 at the market's lowest point in each of those years (perfect timing, which no one has), you'd have accumulated $387,120. If you'd invested the money the day you got it, you'd have done nearly as well, accumulating $362,185. If you'd divided the sum into twelve monthly investments (dollar cost averaging), you'd have ended up with $352,450. As you can see, the important thing is to invest year in and year out.

Take the time to write a summary of your plan in an investment journal or ledger, which you'll keep updated as your portfolio grows in value. List all the reasons you made the investment decisions you made. In the heat of the media and public frenzy that often surrounds the investment market, it's easy to forget why you came up with the plan you did. Having that reminder will keep you from making changes in the heat of the moment based on someone else's investment decisions. A rational plan will overcome the emotion of the market.

Set up a system whereby you can track the progress of your plan. If you follow a simple plan investing in mutual funds of the type John Bogle suggests, you'll get regular reports, which you can track in a simple ledger. Or use investment software to do the same thing. If you're invested for the long haul and have a sound, diversified portfolio, you won't have to check your portfolio every five minutes. Let the day traders, who don't mind losing fortunes or their minds, do that, while you sleep soundly and enjoy your life.

64. Learn to Work the Numbers

If you don't already know how to calculate interest rates, this is an important skill you need so you can quickly and easily track your investments.

Even though you may be using financial software to keep track of your investment portfolio, you'll find it helpful to understand how to calculate interest rates and compounded growth (increase in value caused by reinvestment of dividends and interest income) affect your bottom line. Here is the basic formula for figuring out approximately what a certain amount of money, invested at a certain rate, over a certain period of time will grow to if the interest it earns is reinvested.

If you were to take $10,000 and put it into a mutual fund that increased in value 10 percent per year, at the end of the first year, if the 10 percent were compounded (reinvested), you'd have roughly $11,000 ($10,000 × 1.10% = $11,000).

At the end of the second year, you'd have roughly $12,100 ($11,000 × 1.10% = $12,100).

At the end of the third year, you'd have roughly $13,310 ($12,100 × 1.10% = $13,310).

If you continue making that calculation over twenty years, you'll reach a total of roughly $67,000.

Over thirty years it would be worth roughly $175,000.

Over forty years it would be worth roughly $450,000.

If you were to take the $10,000 and invest it in a mutual fund and, in addition to reinvesting the 10 percent investment return each year, you also added another $1,000 per year, in twenty years you'd end up with nearly double the $67,000, or approximately $130,000 ($10,000 + $1,000 = $11,000 × 1.10% and so on, repeated over 20 years equals roughly $130,000).

If you added 10 percent of each year's *ending* value, rather than 10 percent of the beginning value as shown here, the account would grow to roughly $450,000 over twenty years.

Now, of course, there are no stock, bond, or mutual fund investments that will consistently earn 10 percent year in and year out for twenty, thirty, or forty years. Some years you might, if you're very lucky, have a 25 percent or more return. (The best year for the Standard & Poor's 500 during the past fifty years was 1954 at 52.6 percent.) Other years might yield a loss. (The S&P return for 1974, the worst year during the past fifty years, was a minus 26.5 percent.) In fact, the 10 percent figure used in the calculations above and throughout this part is somewhat conservative: The average S&P 500 return for the past fifty years is 13.6 percent.

Also, of course, the above examples do not reflect investment costs (the fees charged by stock brokers, brokerage houses, and mutual fund managers), nor do they reflect the difference you would see if you invested money each month versus each year. Nor does it reflect the percentage lost because of taxes. (Though if this $10,000 were held in a qualified retirement plan, the value would not begin to be eroded by taxes until you started withdrawing the income after you retire. At that time, presumably your tax rate would be lower than it is in your higher-income-earning years. The real value of a qualified retirement plan is that it defers the taxes so that you have a higher amount invested each year on which to earn a return.)

You can see that the numbers shown here are only approximations. But they demonstrate the benefits of leaving an investment in place over a long period of time, reinvesting the earnings each year, and increasing the percentage invested annually. Obviously, the more money you invest each year, especially in the early years, the higher the amount you'll have, all other things being equal, at the end of twenty, thirty, or forty years.

You can use a financial software program to calculate these numbers. And, again, I encourage you to do that. Once you've learned the process, either on a calculator or with financial software, take the time to explore numerous scenarios (increasing or decreasing the amount you invest, increasing or decreasing the number of years you hold the investment, changing the percentage of increase up or down over the years, and so forth). The software will be lightning fast and will also likely be more accurate than using a calculator.

By working the numbers backward and forward, you'll quickly see why it pays to pay yourself first year in and year out, to start early and stay in for the long haul, and to leave the principal alone.

65. Don't Touch the Principal

The three most important steps you can take to achieve financial independence are: (1) figure out what your means are and learn to live within them; (2) set aside a portion of those means as a principal sum that is invested long-term; and (3) don't touch the principal. The most important of these steps is don't touch the principal. You can set aside money till the cows come home, but if you continue to dip into it, you'll never achieve financial independence.

Webster's Dictionary defines principal as "the capital sum as distinguished from the interest or income on it." The 20 percent or more you set aside each month for retirement is your principal, your capital sum. This principal, when invested, earns its own income, which, when reinvested, also becomes principal. It is this total principal sum that will generate a retirement income when you no longer can or choose to earn income through employment. All financially independent people know that the principal is sacred, never to be tapped into for any reason.

My friend Jean inherited $50,000 when she was forty-five years old. She was a single mother with two sons, one in high school, the other in college. She'd been self-employed in a small retail business for many years, and though she was well on the way to owning her own home, she'd never set any money aside for her retirement years. She had minimal savings and could look forward to only the bare minimum of social security benefits when she retired.

When this $50,000 windfall fell into her lap, I strongly urged her to think of it as principal and to invest it for the long term in a couple of growth-oriented mutual funds so she'd have an income stream to add to her social security benefits when the time came for her to retire.

Understandably, she was not enamored with this idea. Her older son needed a new car, and she wanted to landscape her front yard and join a health club. This money made it possible for her to do that, as well as to acquire a number of things she'd never had the opportunity to purchase. She's now almost sixty years old. She doesn't have a single dollar left of that $50,000. Other than a nicely landscaped front yard, she has nothing to show for her inheritance.

Had she socked that $50,000 away at the time in a growth-oriented mutual fund and had simply let it grow, it could easily be worth close to $250,000 today.

Even if she had invested only half of it, that $25,000 would be worth significantly more than she has now.

You can do the calculation yourself to figure out what $25,000 or $50,000 would be worth had she invested it and added $100 a month over the last fourteen years at a conservative—for the recent market—return of 10 percent.

My dad never earned more than $400 a month during his entire working life. Yet when he died in 1978 at the age of seventy-two, he owned his own home free and clear and left a nest egg that made it possible for my mother to live in comfort for the next twenty years. My mother spent the last year of her life in a managed care facility, but there was enough left over when she died to provide her three kids a modest inheritance.

How did they do this? Like all financially independent people, they didn't touch the principal. Even when, at the age of forty-four, Dad fell off a ladder, broke his arm, and was unable to continue his work as a painting contractor until his arm healed, they didn't touch the principal. We lived on contingency savings through the winter until he was able to return to work.

When we kids were out of the house, Mom joined the workforce, and they were able to increase the amount they added to the principal each month. For years they lived within his income and invested every penny of hers. When their home started to need repairs and replacement of major appliances, they didn't touch the principal. They tapped into their contingency savings when they could or went without when they couldn't.

Though my parents weren't millionaires, they were able to achieve financial independence and to have control of their financial lives until they died. They did this simply by allowing the principal to grow untouched.

Once you've got the principal set aside and working for you, I urge you to pretend that it's double locked behind steel doors, inaccessible until you retire.

66. Figure Out Other Ways to Add to Your Principal

If you're late getting started in a program for building financial security, you might be concerned that if you're setting aside only 20 percent of your after-tax income, it will not grow quickly enough to create the nest egg you need when you retire. If that's the case, here are some ways to add to your retirement wealth-building fund.

- Don't spend your next raise or the one after that. Calculate the difference your next raise will add to your bottom line after taxes, then arrange to have that amount automatically deducted from your paycheck and put it into your qualified retirement plan or separate retirement fund.
- Do the same with your next bonus.
- Take your next vacation at home or near home. Figure out what you can do to have an enjoyable time off with your family without having to spend lots of money on airfares and other expensive accommodations. Put the money you save, or a significant portion of it, into your retirement fund.

- If you get a tax refund, put it into your retirement fund.

- If you receive a repayment on an old debt, put it into your retirement fund.

- Figure out creative ways to reduce your holiday gift spending. The average family spends upward of $1,300 each holiday season. This amount goes on credit cards, and it can take eight months or more to pay off. Never go into debt for something you put under a Christmas tree.

- If you know you'll be receiving an inheritance or any other significant sum of money, put all or most of it into your retirement fund.

- If you know your monthly PITI (principle, interest, taxes, insurance) payment is more than you can comfortably afford, seriously consider moving to a more affordable home. If you have enough equity in your present home to put a larger down payment on a less expensive home and thereby significantly reduce your monthly payment, take a portion of what you save on your monthly PITI payment and add it to your retirement fund each month.

- If you have enough equity to own a less expensive home free and clear with cash left over, put a significant portion of that excess equity into your wealth-building retirement fund and watch it grow.

- Take a moment right now to see how you could either reduce your spending or in any other way make larger contributions to your retirement money. Then work the numbers to determine the difference this makes to your long-term financial security.

67. Put It All Together

There are numerous things you can do to achieve financial security.

- You could be born into money and know how to hold on to it.
- You could win the lottery and learn how to keep it, though most people don't win, and when they do, they don't keep it.
- You could cash in your shares in the company you've been working to build.
- You could start your own business and hit it big.
- You could follow the steps I outline in this part.

Next to being born with money and learning how to keep it, the plan outlined in this part is perhaps the most certain way to achieve financial security and even financial independence.

The steps, once again, are fairly straightforward:

- Take the time to figure out what your true after-tax income actually is, and learn to live within it.

- Understand the time value of money so you'll fully understand the benefits of investing a portion of your after-tax income and staying invested without raiding the principal.

- Keep your monthly housing expense within your means, and avoid buying anything but your house and your car that you can't pay in full by the end of the month.

- Don't let someone else dictate how much money you can afford to spend on your home, car, or anything else.

- Know that achieving financial security through long-term investing is really quite simple. The most certain way to succeed is to figure out how to do it yourself, even if you make some mistakes along the way, and to never let someone else manage your money for you.

- If you're late getting started, you'll increase your chances of success if you figure out various ways to add to your principal as early in the game as possible.

Of course, there's always the danger that you'll get so good at saving money that you never learn how to spend it wisely when you do have it or, worse yet, never learn how to enjoy it. We've all read about people who scrimped and saved and lived frugally and even stingily until the day they died, then left an estate worth millions to their cat (though most people would probably agree that it's better to die with money than to run out of money before you die). The best plan of all is to spend your last dime, then drop dead, though doing that takes expert timing that few of us have.

You've seen that working longer hours will not necessarily help you become financially secure. Yes, it might make it possible to advance in your career and thereby earn more money, but if you're not taking the time to figure out how to spend less than you earn and to make sure that you have an investment plan in place for your retirement dollars, working more to earn more money won't help you much in the long run. Someone who earns $200,000 a year but spends $250,000 a year is far less "wealthy" than someone who earns $50,000 and lives on $40,000, saving and investing the difference.

Take building financial security seriously, but not so seriously that you forget to enjoy your life. Make sure you take the time to do the things you love to do. In the beginning—and even in the end—remember that the best things in life are free; they cost nothing but the time to enjoy them.

So, as in all areas of life, when it comes to financial planning, don't forget to cultivate balance.

SIX

Changing the Way You Work

68. Find a Worker-Friendly Environment

As we've seen, thousands of Americans are starting to rethink their work habits. But workers are not the only ones who are wising up. Literally hundreds of businesses have made major changes in the work environment they offer their employees. Many of these, with branches all around the country, are Fortune 500 companies such as AT&T, Bank of America, American Express, General Motors, DuPont, Eastman Chemical, Aetna, Allstate Insurance, J. P. Morgan, Texas Instruments, Nordstrom, Lucent Technologies, IBM, and Xerox, to name just a few. And hundreds of smaller companies are making changes, too.

One way to simplify your work life is to lobby your current employer to establish employee-friendly policies or, if that's not possible, to find a company that already has them in place. As recently as five years ago, employees mostly ignored corporate-sponsored programs for cutting back. In many companies either subtle pressure from management or peer pressure practically guaranteed that anyone taking advantage of flex schedules, job sharing, or other such options would be passed over for raises or promotions. Saying you wanted to cut back to a balanced work schedule was tantamount to saying you couldn't cut it in a high-pressure workplace.

But all that is rapidly changing. Not only have many companies instituted training classes for managers and employees so they understand these new programs and how they can best be used by workers, but also many have tied executives' compensation to the usage and results of these programs. Just think about this: *Managers are getting paid to make certain their staff takes advantage of the flexible work programs companies are now offering.* This is revolutionary.

And the number of companies offering family-friendly programs in the form of fully paid maternity leave and phase-back periods for both moms and dads is growing every year. Lactation programs, adoption aid, and on-site day-care centers for preschool as well as school-age kids are sprouting up in companies around the country. Others offer before- and after-school care, backup care, and sick-child care. An increasing number of companies have expanded dependent care benefits to include elder care as well as child care.

In addition, many companies are providing other services to

make their employees' lives easier, including everything from company gyms and fitness centers, wellness centers, free- or at-cost lunch programs to emergency backup child care, company-paid counseling and guidance services, and even shopping and delivery services.

Not only are these companies offering attractive compensation, insurance, profit sharing, company-paid pensions, stock purchase plans, and free medical insurance, many are footing the cost of undergraduate or graduate study to help employees advance in their careers.

Yet as important and revolutionary as these things are, they are not enough. Many companies are also realizing that in order to attract and keep good people, they have to offer what workers really want today: a worker- and family-friendly atmosphere where it's possible to have a satisfying job, a balanced lifestyle, and opportunity for advancement. And more and more companies are doing just that.

Obviously, these changes have not come about because of corporate altruism. Companies have figured out that family-friendly policies have the power to attract and keep talented and accomplished people. They've also learned how expensive it is to train new employees to replace those who've left for greener pastures, which thousands of employees are now not hesitating to do. But beyond that, the number crunchers know that over the long haul, job performance, commitment to the company, productivity, and profits increase when employees are not worked beyond endurance. It's also a matter of corporate survival; as long as companies are facing labor shortages, they're forced to take radical means to attract and keep employees.

If you're thinking of moving to a more employee-friendly company, I invite you to check out the *Working Mother* magazine Web site, workingmother.com, for a list of the hundred best companies not just for working moms but for dads and single people, too. You can use this list to find a company in your field that recognizes your value and contribution to its own goals as well as recognizing your responsibility to your family. You can also use this list as a way to begin the process of changing the conditions in your present working environment.

In businesses large and small all across the country, thousands of employees are taking advantage of corporate policies that make it possible for them to cut back. Make sure you get on this bandwagon.

69. Consider the Options

Not long ago there were only three work options: full-time work, part-time work, and no work. If you wanted to establish a career path, there was only one option: full time. If you chose to put in twenty hours a week instead of forty, you were automatically relegated to the no-growth track. (In fact, in many industries, you were put on the no-growth path if you chose to put in only forty hours a week.) And of course, with less than forty hours, you received none of the benefits of full-time workers, such as health insurance, pensions, and vacation time.

Until recently this inability to advance has been a special problem for working moms who wanted to be available for their children, for those who were juggling work and school, and for those who have long recognized the need for balance in their lives. Taking time off for almost any reason—to have a baby, to take a sabbatical, to go back to school, or to smell the roses—would have jeopardized future success. Those were the dark ages when commitment and productivity were measured by the hours you put in. My friend Sally still remembers working, very briefly, for a boss who liked to chide staffers who dared to leave before 7 P.M. by saying "I see you're working another half day."

Now the choices for those who choose to work less than full time are greatly expanded. Recently I heard from a reader named Margaret, a thirty-five-year-old woman working for a private charity in Washington, D.C. When Margaret and her husband decided to have a child, she planned to return to work at the end of her six-week maternity leave. However, as her pregnancy progressed, she realized she wasn't going to be happy leaving her newborn in the care of others five days a week. She and her husband decided they could afford for Margaret to work part time for a year, and her company was agreeable. But Margaret wasn't entirely happy with the solution. She'd invested so much in her career, and she feared that as a part-timer, she'd be out of the loop.

But it turned out that Joan, a woman in Margaret's division, was also pregnant, and she too was concerned about losing her place on her career track if she cut back on her work schedule after her maternity leave. It dawned on them that if they could share their job, both their problems would be solved. Their job descriptions were the same and they already shared many assignments. So they sat down and figured out the logistics of how they would divide the hours, responsibilities, and compensation. They decided that each would work five days during every two-week pay period—three days one week and two days the next. The more they explored the possibilities, the more it became clear that job sharing would benefit everyone involved.

"Our company was supportive because what we proposed not only solved our individual problems but also solved the company's problem, too," Margaret said. "Our plan was to function as a team, so that one of us would always be available. If we'd both been working part time on our own, there would have been less continuity and accessibility. We convinced our managers that they'd be getting two for the price of one. And, in fact, we've found that two heads are better than one. Together we've come up with solutions to several challenges that neither one of us would have been able to come up with on our own."

Creative approaches like this have led many companies to conclude that flexibility is not just something to be tolerated but a policy to be embraced. In fact, companies are starting to extend medical, dental, and other benefits similar to those enjoyed by full-timers to job sharers.

Yes, there are still many companies where flexibility is not yet an option. But emerging trends in the workplace suggest that we are entering a new era where companies are open to ideas that make it possible for their employees to live more meaningful, fulfilled lives.

70. Create Your Own Options

My primary care physician is a thirty-eight-year-old mother of two boys, three and seven. She has established a successful medical practice working part time so she can be available to her children and her husband. She made the decision from the beginning of her career that she would arrange her time so she could see patients, have the time to keep up with her professional reading, and make time for the family she knew she wanted to have. In addition to creating that option for herself, having her own practice made it possible for her to offer her staff flexible schedules, as well, something she was committed to.

Her husband has his own accounting practice, and he too works less than full time, arranging his appointments around his wife's schedule so that one of them is always there for their kids. They've created what is the best of both worlds for many working couples: Each of them has a satisfying career, and they have time to be with their kids and with each other. They've broken the mold.

It's true, they don't live in a palatial mansion of the type usually associated with a physician's income. They live in a modest neighborhood, and neither drives a brand-new car. But they know what their priorities are, and they've arranged their lives accordingly.

My accountant did something similar. When he and his wife divorced, he got custody of their ten-year-old son. For the next eight years Mike set up his accounting practice so he was home when his son got home from school. It was standard policy in his office that if his son called, the call was to be put through to Mike, no matter whom he was with. He simply arranged his life so that there was never a time when his son needed him that he was not available. Most of his clients not only adapted to Mike's schedule, they also admired his dedication to his family. If they didn't, Mike preferred they go elsewhere.

Now that his son is in college, Mike continues to work a flexible schedule. He works hard, though not too hard, during tax season, then makes sure he has plenty of time off during the rest of the year. He maintains the free time he grew accustomed to through the years of raising his son. Again, his home is, as he calls it, a shack. But it's near the beach in one of the most beautiful areas of the world. He's not done too badly working a flexible schedule.

In countless professions and lines of work, a flex schedule is a realistic and viable option for earning a good living while enjoying the good life. As one professional journalist who spent twenty years on the fast track with a major newsmagazine recently wrote to me, "Both my husband [a former investment banker] and I decided to cut back our long hours and arrange our lives so we could work at home. We finally realized we had the choice of having gobs of money but no time, or of having enough money and scads of time. We opted for scads of time, and we've never looked back. Now I never spend a moment worrying whether I'm doing the right thing for my family."

71. Look at What Companies Are Doing to Be Flexible

In its 1999 annual survey of the best companies for working mothers, *Working Woman* magazine found that every single one of the hundred companies chosen offers at least one flexible working arrangement.

For example, Gannett Media's technical group in Wichita, Kansas, allows employees to set their own schedules as long as all shifts are covered. They use a combination of four-day weeks, part-time hours, and multiple shifts.

American Home Products allows sales reps to work less than nineteen hours a week and to choose their own schedule.

Many companies are now allowing parents to bring a child to the office for the day when the need arises and to take off up to twelve weeks during the summer months to be with their kids.

Cigna has more than six hundred high-ranking executives, managers, and professionals who work part time, and three thousand employees work from home at least one day a week.

First Union Bank offers employees, in addition to the standard vacation days, ten annual days of family care leave for tending to an ill spouse, parent, or child.

Fleet Financial Group offers every employee a flexible schedule now that the company realized that managers with flexible schedules generated $16 million more in new business than their full-time counterparts.

After figuring out that their employees' greatest need was for flexibility, GenAmerica Insurance Company executives instituted alternative work arrangements that include flex time, compressed workweeks, job sharing, and part-time work in order to make their company more competitive.

Many companies now offer not only local but also long-distance telecommuting.

Many companies offering a formal flex schedule also offer job guarantees, something practically unheard of in corporate America even five years ago. IBM offers mothers and fathers three years of job-guaranteed time off. Procter & Gamble has expanded its reduced-workweek policy, which originally allowed parents to work part time for up to five years following the birth of a child while keeping their same jobs; now any parents can go part time and stay on a reduced schedule as long as they wish.

GTE, in addition to generous time-off programs for new moms, also offers time-off for new grandparents.

USWest Telecommunications offers numerous flexible work options, including their innovative "Securids," which allows 22,000 of its employees to access their workstations from a remote location.

Household International has expanded its flex schedule by allowing employees to buy or sell days off in their paid time-off bank.

At Lancaster Laboratories every single employee uses flex time and 26 percent work at home on an as-needed basis.

Eli Lilly has made job sharing easier by adding a work/life Web site that includes an interactive database that helps workers locate job share partners.

Patagonia offers a two-month paid sabbatical for employees who want to take time off to work for a nonprofit environmental organization.

And talk about flexibility, an enforced biweekly no-meetings day might be reason enough for anyone to quit a job and go to work for Johnson Wax.

72. Sell Your Boss on Telecommuting

Telecommuters are the fastest-growing segment of the work-at-home movement. When I talk to people who telecommute one or two days a week, almost all of them have the same comment: "I get so much more work done without the distractions of the office." It's ironic that the office is often the most difficult place to be productive, but many of us have experienced this. Also, 90 percent of telecommuters say that telecommuting has helped them balance their work lives with their personal lives.

According to the American Telecommuting Association, telecommuting can benefit everyone involved.

The individual benefits by eliminating the cost, time, and stress involved in commuting to work. This translates into more discretionary time, greater flexibility, and an overall feeling of control.

The family benefits from having Mom or Dad around for that extra hour or two each day—without the frustration and anxiety that follows the evening commute home.

Society benefits because telecommuting cuts down on air pollution, use of nonrenewable energy sources, and traffic congestion.

The employer benefits by having happier, more productive workers. There's also a cost savings. If half the workforce telecommutes even one day a week, a company can reduce its overhead by 10 percent.

However, despite the recent increase in the number of people who telecommute and the incredible advantages telecommuting offers to both employees and employers, the benefits aren't always apparent to bosses. Many managers fear that out of sight means out of mind for workers. If you'd like to make the shift to telecommuting for part of your workweek, you may need to sell your boss on the benefits.

If your boss needs convincing, here are some of the most common objections and suggested responses you can give:

Objection: I can't be sure people are working unless I actually see them busy at their desks.

Response: There are much better ways to measure productivity than observation. Simply agree on the goals and expectations, the time line, and a method of accountability.

Objection: Telecommuting is a good deal for the worker but not for the organization.

Response: Telecommuting can be very profitable for an organization. It cuts overhead, increases productivity, and makes for happier, more loyal employees. Workers who telecommute are strongly motivated to do well in order to keep the privilege, and many companies find employees are much more willing to go the extra mile out of simple gratitude for the flexibility telecommuting offers them.

Objection: It takes office contact to stimulate new ideas, creativity, professionalism and high levels of energy.

Response: That's partly true. But with today's vast and efficient communication technologies, people are interacting more and more across spatial boundaries. In fact, we're rapidly building a more mental, and less physical, world of work.

The American Telecommuting Association is a great resource for companies that need information and support initiating telecommuting efforts. Contact them at 1220 L Street NW, Suite 100, Washington, DC 20005; 1-800-ATA-4-YOU; www.knowledgetree.com.

Before you approach your boss about telecommuting, be sure to take the time to think through your proposal—from your specific goals to the practical organizational issues, like accountability and company interactions. If telecommuting is a foreign concept in your company, start modestly. Suggest a trial of one day a week for three months, and choose the day that is least disruptive for the office. Do everything you can to prove that this is a sound, profitable plan. Your reward will be the opportunity to enjoy more freedom and to replace your commute with quality time.

For an excellent guide that will help you decide if you're the telecommuting type, provide other ways to convince your boss that telecommuting is in everyone's best interests, and show you how to best arrange your office and your life for telecommuting, read Alice Bredin's book *The Virtual Office Survival Handbook: What Telecommuters and Entrepreneurs Need to Succeed in Today's Nontraditional Workplace* (Wiley, 1996).

73. Make Sure You're Suited to Work at Home

According to the U.S. Department of Labor, more than 12 million Americans work part time or full time from their homes. That's one worker out of every eleven. Working at home is a growing trend that shows every sign of becoming even more significant, thanks to new technologies.

I love having a home office and working for myself. It suits me perfectly. I've worked at home for over twenty years, and now I can't imagine working for someone else. I'm fortunate that the work I love to do allows me to choose the environment and schedule that is best for me.

But keep in mind that not everyone is suited temperamentally to work at home. It may sound wonderful when you're chained to a desk in an office, or enduring the rush-hour crawl on the freeway, but if you're considering shifting to a home office, you might want to engage in some serious thought to make sure it's right for you.

Be aware of the common pitfalls. For example, there is an annoying tendency for neighbors, friends, and telemarketers to assume that if you're home during the day, you're free to chat, run errands, help out at school or church, be available to pinch-hit in emergencies, and listen to sales pitches. This was one of the biggest challenges when I first started working at home. Even now with telecommuting so prevalent, people often still assume that if you're at home, you're not working. It took me quite a while to educate my friends and family otherwise.

This assumption isn't made just for women. A man I know who works from home as an independent contractor for a pharmaceutical company recently found himself baby-sitting for a neighbor across the street while she ran an errand that stretched into two hours. He confessed he didn't know how to say no when she asked him to do her the favor. I asked him how he'd have felt if his neighbor had walked into his previous place of employment and made the same request. Of course, he laughed at the very idea. If you're going to work from home, be prepared to set serious boundaries and be brutal about saying no.

In addition to educating your friends and neighbors, be prepared to educate your kids and perhaps even your spouse. Before you start working at home, draw up a set of rules for the family and stick with them. This is especially important if you're combining a home-based business with child raising. It's also important to keep in mind that having a home-based office is not a substitute for child or elder care.

Also be aware that some people have a terrible time staying focused on their work when they're doing it at home. The garden beckons, the dishes and laundry clamor to be done, their eyes are drawn to the dust motes under the desk. There are literally hundreds of temptations to do anything else but work. You must be seriously disciplined, especially if you're easily distracted. Many people working at home find it helps to keep set hours and, if space allows, set their office apart in some way.

A writer friend of mine found that working from his home office become much easier when he sealed off the door to the rest of the house and cut a new entrance to the office from the deck. Having to "leave" home each morning to get to his office made the psychological difference for him.

One woman I know initially loved the freedom of being able to stay in her bathrobe all morning. The problem was that she had trouble getting things done because mentally she was still in a relaxation mode. It was only when she got dressed first thing in the morning that she found the energy and motivation to get down to business.

People who've worked in offices for many years sometimes

don't appreciate how much they relied on the daily camaraderie with coworkers. They miss the regular give-and-take and find that the telephone and e-mail don't provide the level of connection they need. Take an honest look at your need to have other people around you to see if you could survive without the presence of others.

Read *101 Tips for Telecommuters* by Debra A. Dinnocenzo (Berrett/Koehler Publishers, 1999) for dozens of helpful ideas on how to manage your work, your team, your family, and technology if you decide to work at home.

74. Decide If You Can Afford to Work

Whenever I ask people if they can get by on less income, they say I must be kidding. As we've seen, most people today are stretched to their financial limits and beyond. Their needs tend to expand to match their income until they truly can't see how they could survive with less. What they often fail to see is just how much it costs to go to work every day.

If you dream of working part time or trying a job-sharing arrangement so you can spend more time with your kids, go back to school, or get started on the novel you've longed to write, it may not be as big a shock to your budget as you think. Let's do the math.

First, add up all the expenses that are a direct result of your job. These include child care, transportation, food, uniforms, and taxes. Subtract the total from your monthly net income.

Now add up all the expenses that are an indirect result of your job. These include wardrobe items; a briefcase; a Palm Pilot or reasonably sophisticated time management system; perhaps a portable computer and other electronic gear; a cell phone and monthly phone bills; dry cleaning; designer coffees, frequent drinks, lunches, and dinners with coworkers; office gift collections, party contributions, and the like. You might be surprised by how much you're spending on these items. It's a lot of work and expense to keep an office-worthy wardrobe in good condition.

Now subtract your total indirect expenses from the subtotal.

I once did this exercise with a woman who wanted to stay home with her baby for a year but swore that she and her husband couldn't survive without her income. She made $40,000 a year, but by the time she'd subtracted all of the costs of working, she found her true salary was $883 a month. I asked her, "If an employer offered you a full-time job for a salary of $883 a month, what would you say?" She laughed and replied, "I'd say, 'You're out of your mind,' especially since I work well beyond forty hours a week."

Also keep in mind that not all of the expenses of working can be measured in dollars and cents. There are also the emotional, mental, and spiritual costs of being consumed by work. I suspect that the so-called midlife crisis so many people experience is mostly due to the sense that the real joys of life are passing them by while they're busy keeping their noses to the grindstone.

Ask yourself: "Why am I working so hard?" Then try to answer honestly. For example:

"I'm working so hard so the family can afford a nice vacation." Maybe that expensive vacation wouldn't be necessary if you weren't working so hard.

"I'm working so hard to put my kids in private schools." Have you looked at other options? There are many independent and charter schools that provide excellent educations but that require active parental participation. It's possible that if you weren't working so hard, you could be more personally involved in seeing that your kids get the education you want them to have.

"I'm working so hard to afford my house, car, furniture, etc." How important will it be to your kids in the long run if you never have the time to be with them, or to be there for them when they need you, or to simply enjoy the home you're spending so much time paying for?

Today's working world offers unlimited possibilities for anyone who wants to take advantage of them. If you take the time to figure out how to make changes in the way you work, you simply don't have to work as hard or long as you have been. If you have the opportunity to add balance, purpose, and new meaning to your life, ask yourself if you can afford not to take advantage of it.

75. Start Your Own Business

How often have you looked with envy on a small business owner and thought, "I could do that"? Owning your own business, setting your own rules, creating your own opportunities has long been considered the American dream. Self-employed people make up less than 20 percent of the workers in America but account for two-thirds of the millionaires. As industries and corporations have grown vaster and more remote, many people long for a more direct connection with the work they do. Small, personally owned businesses or a home-based business can enable us to put the meaning back into work and give the numbed and burned out workforce something personally enriching to strive for.

Today, as we enter a new millennium, becoming a small business owner or having our own home-based business is a realistic possibility; for many it may be a necessity as companies are outsourcing white-collar tasks to independent contractors and to workers in other countries. According to the U.S. Small

Business Administration, the number of small businesses is growing at a rate of about 1 million per year, and the rate is comparable for home-based businesses. There are currently 25 million small businesses in the country, and these are responsible for 75 percent of all new jobs—especially for younger workers, older workers, women, and part-time workers. It's a healthy picture.

If you're serious about starting your own business, here are some things to think about:

1. Define your passion. Maybe you haven't figured out exactly what you want to do, and think you could be just as happy in any number of different business ventures. Or you may have a lifelong dream of running a day care center or owning a bookstore or pastry shop, or becoming a consultant to your industry. No matter which profile you fit, be sure to choose something that will make you eager to get out of bed every morning.

2. Find a need. The fundamental role of business is to meet a real need. I know a woman who started a company that sold gift certificates for various services—housecleaning, personal shopping, and errand running. She based her idea on two facts: (1) that women, who usually perform those tasks, were busier than ever; and (2) that men usually

had a terrible time coming up with gift ideas for their partners. It was a perfect match of service to need.

3. Do your budget. What are your start-up costs? Do you need to hire staff? What about taxes, pensions, and health benefits? Are you going to need a small business loan? Will your earnings be seasonal or year-round? How long will it take to make a profit? Get as much support as possible. Browse the Small Business Administration's Web site (www.sba.gov) for useful information and to find resources in your area. Sometimes people forget to ask the government for help, and the SBA is one of the most proactive agencies when it comes to offering small businesses the tools they need to succeed.

   While you're at it, take the SBA's quiz to determine your best business profile and road to success. Another great organization is the National Association for the Self-Employed. Check out their Web site (www.NASE.com) to read articles from their magazine archives, or call their toll-free helpline (800-232-6273) for advice on everything from tax deductions to moving your business out of the house. The NASE Web site also offers links to dozens of other small business–related Web sites.

4. Determine the personal impacts. How will owning a business change your life—in the short term and the long term? How will it change your family's life? What sacrifices will you have to make to get your

business up and going? Are these sacrifices worth it? How do you see yourself living five or ten years down the road?

5. Be prepared for dramatic changes in the marketplace as technology and the global economy reinvent the world of work as we know it. This is one more reason to simplify your work life: So you can keep up with how the world of work is changing, figure out what you need to spend your time doing, decide what really matters, and adapt accordingly. Your success will depend on your ability to determine a need, then being prepared to change as the needs of your market change.

Initially, starting your own business may not seem like the best way to simplify your life. It can get pretty harried. But when you work hard at something that has personal meaning for you, your life seems easier. I've spoken to countless small business owners, and I know from my own experience that working on your own terms changes how you view what you do every day. You may work longer hours with more intensity, but the load feels lighter.

76. Find a Coach

It can be lonely at the top—and that's especially true when you're starting your own business. Don't make the mistake of thinking you have to figure everything out on your own. Be aggressive about looking for people whose wisdom and experience you trust. Do your homework. Form your own support group of small business owners or join an existing group to keep abreast of the latest tax law changes and other factors that could affect your business.

Whether you have your own business or are working for someone else, you might also want to consider hiring a coach who can help you achieve your goals. Business and executive coaches have become increasingly common in just about every field of endeavor.

In sports, a coach is your mentor, your advisor, your advocate, and the one who motivates you to be the best you can be. The same is true of a business coach. A good coach can help simplify your business life by cutting through the brush and defining a clear direction, then helping you achieve your full potential in following that direction. A good coach works with your personal development, not just your business goals. A good coach can help you articulate your goals, eliminate the barriers that are getting in your way, and guide you on a path to success and satisfaction.

Where can you find a coach, and how do you know if that person is right for you? With more than 10,000 full- and part-time business coaches operating in the United States, you have plenty to choose from. However, because it's an evolving field, there are no clearly established rules about standards, fees, and practices. Business coaches can come from a variety of back-grounds. Sometimes they're former business owners themselves. Sometimes they're psychologists. Often they're former teachers. Here are some thoughts about how to make the right choice.

If you've never used a coach before, start by contacting the International Coach Federation in Washington, DC. The Web address is www.coachfederation.com. You can also call 202-712-9039 or 888-423-3131. The Coach Federation develops tools for coaches, hosts an annual convention, and sponsors a referral service. Another good resource is Corporate Coaches, Inc., which sponsors CoachU, a training and certification center for coaches. Their Web site is www.coachu.com.

Many coaches have Web pages, and you can pick up helpful information by browsing through them. Usually these sites explain a coach's philosophy, working style, programs, and fees. You'll start to get a sense of what's typical and what you particularly like.

Check your local phone directory yellow pages or the classified section of your newspaper. Also, put out the word to people you know that you are looking for a good coach. Word of mouth is sometimes the best way to connect with the right person.

Before you interview a potential coach, get a clear picture of what you hope to gain from the association. Determine which coaching style will work best for you. Do you want help developing a targeted business plan, or are you more interested in general help with meeting your life goals both personally and professionally? Do you prefer to work face to face or over the phone? Are you looking for a short-term relationship to get you started or a long-term association?

Trust your instincts about the coaches you interview. A good coach isn't just someone with the right credentials. A good coach must also be someone with whom you have a strong rapport, as well as shared values. For example, if your goal is to simplify your work life, you need a coach who embraces this goal and knows how to help you fulfill it.

Ask the coach you're interested in hiring to draft a proposal for a working arrangement that suits your goals, budget, and time. Request a list of client references, and be sure to check them. Also check with all your senses (#36) to make sure the person you're considering is right for you.

You don't necessarily have to hire a professional coach in order to get the benefits of coaching. Maybe you have a former boss or colleague who once served as your mentor and is still willing to advise you. Or you might find a retired small business owner in your community who would be happy to serve as a sounding board for your ideas. Many people find great satisfaction in helping others succeed. Often these people are happy to donate their time as a way of paying back their community, or charge only a fraction of what their experience and expertise would bring in the marketplace. If you're lucky enough to know such a person, take advantage of it. If the person you use prefers to donate his or her time, you might someday be able to reciprocate by serving as a coach for someone else just starting out.

SEVEN

Changing the Way You Think

About Work

77. Understand How We Got Here

One thing that was most helpful to me in simplifying my work life was understanding how and why my work schedule had become so complicated to begin with.

Thirty years ago we were asking ourselves what we were going to do with all the leisure time we'd have because of the new technology that would make our lives so much easier. How would we spend all the money the new economy was going to generate? Then, before we knew what had hit us, our workweeks had increased by ten hours or more and the "new economy" had reduced our real wages by 14 percent. What happened?

George Santayana said those who fail to understand the past are doomed to repeat it. So let's take a look at some of the circumstances that shaped our present-day work ethic.

In 1938 Congress passed the Fair Labor Standards Act as part of President Franklin D. Roosevelt's New Deal. With this law, the eight-hour day, and time-and-a-half pay for overtime, became the law of the land for wage workers. This meant that after more than one hundred years of struggle, laborers had finally achieved one of their major objectives: Reducing the number of hours they worked each day and ending many years of overwork and abuse by management.

Unfortunately for the generations of workers that have followed, this law applies only to wage workers; it doesn't apply to salaried, managerial, administrative, and professional workers. This is how management has been able, through subtle and not-so-subtle means, to induce salaried employees to work well beyond the government-mandated forty hours and to avoid paying them for additional time they put in beyond those forty hours.

The pressure to work longer and harder without additional pay was hardly noticeable at first. In the late 1940s and early 1950s, a certain cachet came with being a salaried manager or a staff member. And early on many people in fact did "get ahead" by working long hours. They moved up the ranks of management, became partners, ran divisions, moved into corner offices, and got more raises and more perks—or at least the promise of them. It seemed at the time that there was no end to how far one could go just by working long and hard, and ever-increasing numbers of people wanted to take this fast track to success.

Then in the late 1970s we entered one of the most inflationary periods in recent economic history and encountered a phenomenon most workers had never experienced. The people who followed the first wave of salaried workers had a more difficult time making it. Many people who wanted to get ahead were working the long hours their predecessors had, but the dollars they earned were worth much less. The homes that their managers had bought just a few years earlier for $80,000 now cost $150,000, and everything else followed suit.

Except wages, which have dropped by 14 percent over the past twenty years. From the mid-1980s to the mid-1990s, not only did the income of the average worker not keep pace with inflation, but we entered a period of corporate downsizing. This included huge layoffs, employee cutbacks, and even salary cuts, (except for some CEOs of mega-corporations who earn two hundred times what their average workers earn and whose salaries increased by 5,000 percent due to corporate buyouts). So not only were people along the entire employment spectrum working longer for less money, they were now afraid that if they didn't work longer hours, they'd lose their jobs. Here's when our present-day work ethic really took hold. From the mid-1980s to the mid-1990s, huge numbers of employees were working longer and harder just to tread water, often at multiple part-time jobs without benefits.

Interwoven through all this, of course, was the impact of the women's movement, which put women into the workforce in unprecedented numbers as they sought opportunities to develop their abilities or to excel.

The pressures to continue to work longer and longer work-weeks come from all sides. Management has seen forty-hour-plus workweeks as a way to get the work done and to build profits without having to pay for the additional hours. Financial pressure is ever present and relentless now that it seems to take two people working full time to support the bare minimum of the American dream or in some areas simply to survive. Peer pressure keeps many of us going because we don't want to fall behind the Joneses.

So there was a brief period of time when working long hours increased one's chances of getting ahead, and for some people it still does. There's little question that this work ethic contributed to great expansions within the economy and unprecedented technological development. But now that the work-hard-and-long ethic is deeply ingrained in our culture, we're starting to realize that the rest of our lives have suffered. Many people find they're so busy working they barely have time to live, and yet, once they get hooked on the work-and-spend treadmill, it seems impossible to stop.

As we've seen, it *is* possible to stop, and as more and more of us change the way we work, the pendulum is swinging the other way. In this time of labor shortages and cutthroat competition, workers are realizing that the old ways of working don't benefit them, and companies are figuring out that they must adjust to the changing needs and demands of the workforce. To speed this process along, it's helpful to change the way we think about our work. In this part we'll explore ways to do that.

78. Consider the Insanity

Management is not necessarily always the bad guy; we've all colluded in one way or another with the conditions of our work lives. But many of us are now waking up to the absurdity of the way we've been embracing work to the near exclusion and to the detriment of all the other aspects of our lives. When we step back and take a look at the imbalances that exist, we have to see that much of what we do to earn a living makes no sense anymore.

Does it make sense, for example, to work ten or twelve hours a day to make huge mortgage payments on a home we never have time to enjoy because we're so busy working to pay for it?

Does it make sense to work ten or twelve hours a day to "support" our families in the style to which we want them to become accustomed, when the real support they want and need is our time and attention?

Does it make sense to work such long hours to pay for the

activities our kids are involved in that keep us all so busy we seldom have time to spend together?

Does it make sense to spend irreplaceable hours of our lives each day in commuter traffic, especially when there are now so many alternatives?

Does it make sense to work our fingers to the bone for employers who don't give us a fair share in the company profits our work makes possible, especially when there are companies that do?

Does it make sense to spend a huge portion of our time each year working to pay off credit card debt, which we incurred buying things we don't want or use?

Does it make sense that we allow the technology of cell phones, faxes, beepers, pagers, and the Net—which have the potential to free us—to keep us shackled to our jobs around the clock?

Does it make sense for us to work forty hours or more each week when technology makes it possible to work half that time?

Does it make sense to continue with a work ethic that is outdated and no longer necessary?

When we can honestly answer these questions, we've taken one of the biggest steps toward change, because if these things don't make sense anymore, then it's time to start doing things differently.

79. Rethink Your Belief System

We often complicate our work lives by holding on to outdated belief systems or clinging to beliefs that never had much validity to begin with. Often, as we've seen, we allow the culture or our workplace to shape our beliefs. Sometimes we latch on to beliefs that have been handed down to us from our parents; sometimes we make up our own belief systems; sometimes we don't have any notion how we acquired the ideas we've come to hold as sacred. The times are changing; it's time to change many of our beliefs as well.

For example, you may believe that you have to work sixty or seventy hours a week in order to be successful. But that's just a belief system. There are many people who've achieved tremendous success working forty hours a week or less.

You may believe that it would be impossible for you to support yourself doing what you love. But that's just a belief system.

Many people have arranged their lives so they can earn a living doing work they love.

You may believe that you have to be a millionaire or a multi-millionaire or even a billionaire in order to be happy. But that's just a belief system. There are many people who are not millionaires who are truly happy and content.

You may believe that because of the speed at which technology advances, you can't stop for a minute or you'll fall behind and never be able to catch up. But that's just a belief system. There are many people who stop every day and are more than able to figure out what they need to know and to keep up with it.

You may believe that you'll be successful when your parents or your peers or your boss think you're successful. But that's just a belief system. You are the only one who can decide if you are truly successful.

You may believe that you and your spouse have to work full time in order to support comfortable lifestyles. But that's just a belief system. Many couples have comfortable lifestyles and raise families with one income or two part-time incomes.

You may believe that you have to live in a huge house in a prestigious neighborhood in order to be happy. But that's just a belief system. Many people who live in modest homes in ordinary neighborhoods are happy and fulfilled.

You may believe it's more important to appear to be wealthy than to actually be wealthy. But that's a belief system sponsored by credit card companies and other debt holders who benefit from your desire to buy all the trappings that would make you appear wealthy.

Take a few moments right now to see if you're holding on to any other beliefs that keep you working longer and harder than you'd like. See if there are any outdated ideas that are keeping you from finding your true life's work. You might find it helpful to examine your beliefs from time to time, to make sure they still support what you actually believe and to see if they enable you to live the way you want to live and work the way you want to work.

80. Reinvent Yourself

Be aware that if you've been working long and hard, changing the way you work may feel strange at first. Your briefcase, your late nights, your hours in the office on weekends have been a sort of security blanket. These things have defined in large measure who you are. It's how you've been presenting yourself to the world. So the question you may have to ask when you stop being that person who works so hard is: Who am I?

If you're like most of us, you've probably boasted subtly from time to time about how much you work, the late hours you keep, all the traveling you do. "I can't possibly join you for dinner; I've got that New Product Development project to finish by the first of the month." "I'll be in Chicago next week, then I'm off to London for ten days." "Yeah, the boss asked me to set up the new branch on the coast, so I'll be doing double time for the next year or so." If you've been portraying yourself to the world as someone who works long hours, and now you're ready to change, you may have to reinvent yourself.

Take a moment right now to imagine walking through your front door without that briefcase. See yourself routinely leaving the office early, or not going in to the office on weekends. Imagine yourself regularly having an evening with your family or having a game of tennis with your friends. When you consciously step off the treadmill, your life will be different. You'll no longer be the person who is identified by how much you work.

You'll gradually become someone who's working considerably less than you used to. You'll be someone who now has time to spend with your family. You'll be a person who knows the importance of rest, relaxation, and having time for fun and for contemplation and for exploring the larger questions of the universe. You'll be a role model for all the people around you who want to cut back but don't know where to begin.

You may feel awkward at first. You may not know quite how to describe yourself to others, or what to do with yourself. It's possible your spouse and your kids won't know exactly what to do with you, either. Who is this person? Their lives may have moved on without you in recent years. You may have to get reacquainted.

Keep in mind that you've already reinvented yourself at least half a dozen times. After you got out of school, you gradually let go of being a student and became a member of the workforce. After you married, you let go of being a single person. After you became a parent, you and your spouse were suddenly no longer the carefree couple you had been. When you moved up from being an entry-level worker, you reinvented yourself as a manager or a department head, or as the head of the company. With each new role you went through a period of adjustment in your thinking about who you were. You changed gears, started off in a new direction, and then created a new persona to match.

Now that you're simplifying your work life, you simply reinvent yourself once again. You know who you've been; now you get to figure out who you want to become.

81. Imagine Your Ideal Work Life

Imagine a work life in which you are accomplished, creative, successful, and productive.

Imagine a work life that makes it possible for you to spend time with the people you love.

Imagine a work life in which you are contributing joyously to your colleagues and clients, as well as to your family, your friends, and your community.

Imagine a world in which the work you do fulfills your innate longing for personal and spiritual growth.

Imagine a world in which you are not just going to "work" but where you are engaged in an adventure that makes you and the world we live in a better place.

Imagine a world in which everyone's needs for food, shelter, and survival are met, where we all work together for the benefit of humankind. We have the technological capability to make that happen. All we have to do is collectively decide to use it for that purpose.

Imagine a world in which you're so excited and enthusiastic about the contribution you make through your work that you're naturally teaching your kids that they too can look forward to going into the world to find their heart's true work, where they get educated and trained to work not just to "pay the bills" but to find and make their own unique contribution.

Imagine a world in which we all accept our responsibility to help design social systems that are in keeping with our desire for greater freedom for all.

Imagine a world in which both workers and management have moved beyond the concepts of scarcity and greed.

Imagine a world in which the companies that provide work do so in the context of being socially, culturally, and environmentally responsible.

Imagine a world in which science and technology are used to develop the optimum potential of all life.

It's possible that not all of the things you imagine would happen in our lifetimes, but imagine them anyway. The changes and improvements that have occurred in the workplace in the past few years have happened because there were people who imagined them and made them happen. You have the option of taking advantage of the better working conditions brought about because of those imaginings, and you can begin anew to imagine your own ideal working conditions that will conform to your picture of the ideal way to work. It is out of our imaginings that we create our lives.

Start imagining now. Your imaginings may well provide the conditions in which someone else can bring a dream of a better work life to fruition. That in itself would help to make a better world.

82. Follow the Wish of Your Heart

We each have a unique gift, a special contribution we can make to the world through the work we do. Up until now our work culture made it difficult, if not impossible, for most people to have the time to figure out what their gift is. Or, if they did figure it out, only a very few knew how to break through the work and cultural barriers so their gift could be shared with the world.

But all that is changing dramatically. We're moving rapidly into an information culture in which the possibilities for creative work are seemingly unlimited. We've shaped hundreds of corporations into responding to our needs for worker- and family-friendly workplaces. Millions of us are contributing to the workforce from the comfort of our home-based businesses and being rewarded in innumerable ways for doing so. We have the technology and are developing the spiritual understanding of how to use it so that millions of people are now able to create balanced lives and to free up time to make their contributions to the world.

As psychologist Abraham Maslow's research revealed 30 years ago, all fully-functioning, productive, joyful people have one trait in common: They're doing work they love.

Those who are waking up to this potential know that when you tap into that part of you that is waiting to emerge, when you're contributing from your heart and from your own special talents, there's no fear, there's no greed, there's no holding back. There is so much joy that comes from following the wish of your heart that there's no time for doubt, no time to worry about money, no time to get distracted by things that don't matter. You just know deep down that if you do what you're meant to do, you'll move ahead with full confidence and do the right thing. There's no question about it. Too many people are doing it now for there to be any doubt that we can all do it.

83. Don't Let Anyone Tell You It Can't Be Done

When I first got the idea to write *Simplify Your Life*, I met with a friend who was a marketing guru to get her professional opinion. She is one of these people who has her finger on the pulse of everything that is happening in marketing trends around the world. She told me, "Elaine, I think it's great that you've simplified your life, but I can't imagine anyone would want to read a book about it." So I said to myself, "Okay, perhaps this isn't such a great idea," and I put the idea out of my mind.

A few months later I was in New York having lunch with another friend and her literary agent. The agent, who knew I had written a book on real estate investing, asked me if I had any other books I was thinking of doing. I told her about my idea for *Simplify Your Life*. She suggested that I send her a copy of the proposal and she'd give me her honest opinion. I thought, "Great! This is one of the top literary agents in New York. If anyone can tell me whether this is a good idea or not, she'd be the one."

So I sent her the proposal as soon as I got back to my office. She called me a couple of days later and said, "Elaine, this book will never fly. You're asking people to turn off their televisions, cancel their magazine subscriptions, and stop taking the newspaper! How are you going to promote this thing? No publisher would buy this book."

Naturally I was disappointed. I decided it was time to come to my senses. After all, two experts had said this book would never sell. It was time for me to move on to something else.

But fortunately I'd simplified my life. Fortunately I'd freed up lots of time to think about what I wanted to do next. Fortunately I'd created the time to think and to just listen. And after a while I became certain that I wanted to take the time and write the book, no matter what these experts said. So I called the agent who had handled my real estate book. She loved the idea, and within two weeks two major publishers made offers on the book based on my proposal.

It's now six years later. I've written a book a year for the past six years, all of which have become bestsellers, and between them there are fifty-six foreign translations. I have a nationally syndicated column, and I regularly have speaking engagements talking to groups around the country about how to simplify their lives.

And while all of this is wonderful, the truly wonderful thing for me is that I hear every day from people around the world, thanking me for writing these books and telling me how simplifying changed their lives for the better. I hear over and over again how, because people have simplified, they've been able to create the time to figure out what really matters to them, to make changes in their lives and do the things they're called to do. For a writer, it doesn't get much better than that.

When I think back to that time these two experts told me a book about simplifying would never work, I'm so grateful for two things. First of all, of course, I'm glad they were wrong. Second, I'm so glad I didn't listen to them. I'm so glad that I'd slowed down long enough to listen instead to that inner voice that was guiding me to the next step on my career path, to the next phase of my soul's work.

I believe we all have work that our soul is calling to us to do. The work we are being guided to—if only we listen—is what we should be doing. I believe those things we truly want to do are the things we came here to do. It's when we're doing that work that we're in love. It's when we're doing that work that we have joy in our lives. It's when we're doing that work that we can truly make a difference—in our own lives, in the lives of the people we love, in our communities, and in the world.

So I encourage you to take the time to think about what it would be like for you to get up every morning and spend your day, or most of it, doing the work your soul calls you to do. The best way I know of to get to that point is to start cutting back, so you can figure out what that work is, then arrange your life so you can do it.

84. Take the Leap

Several years ago my friend Marie asked me to talk with her about her work life. She knew that through the process of simplifying, I'd been able to arrange my life so I was doing something I truly love. She wanted to see what she might be able to do to create her ideal work life.

Marie and her husband, Joe, had recently left the corporate world after many years in the computer and aerospace industries. They'd both achieved moderate levels of success, but they'd reached a point where the grind was no longer worth it. They made the decision to eliminate their long freeway commutes, move to a smaller town, and strike out on their own. Joe stayed with his first love, engineering, and started his own consulting business. Marie, unable to take the time at that point to figure out how to do what she truly wanted to do, went into real estate sales. Though they'd set aside money to carry them through, it was tough for both of them at first. The real estate market was flagging and Joe's consulting business, like many entrepreneurial ventures, had its ups and downs.

Within a year or so, Marie was beginning to suffer from the pressure of working long hours at a job that drained her time and energy, that she didn't really enjoy, and that didn't allow her a true expression of her self.

After we'd talked for a bit, Marie finally had to admit that she was miserable in real estate, but she'd become the breadwinner. She found the thought of making yet another change overwhelming. But as we talked further, an exciting option began to unfold. What she truly wanted to do, in her heart of hearts, was go back to school and get her doctorate in art history. And she had a list of reasons as long as her arm explaining why she couldn't possibly do that:

"I'm too old to go back to school."

"It wouldn't be fair to Joe to ask him to support me while I go off and do what I want."

"Even if I could get my Ph.D., who'd hire a new professor in her late forties?"

"I can't afford to quit. We need my income."

I was familiar with these objections because I'd dealt with many similar ones myself when I decided to leave my investment career. If you've ever faced this dilemma, you're probably familiar with all the reasons that keep you from doing what you know you should do.

Over the course of the afternoon and the next several weeks, I outlined a plan that addressed all of Marie's fears and many more. The plan I laid out for Marie is basically the plan I lay out for you in this book. We started with ways she could cut back her work schedule to give her more time to think about taking the direction she wanted to take. Marie was already fairly adept at setting boundaries, but we spent several hours talking about how she and Joe could handle the financial challenges of her working less or working differently. We also talked about how easy it is in the short term to stay with work we don't love, but the price we pay for that in the long run is devastating.

Marie eventually placed a call to the admissions office of the local university, which offered the program she wanted. Now, six years later, she's charging ahead with her doctoral dissertation. She has received numerous grants and financial awards that she hadn't imagined were possible—which made the financial challenge easier—and she has excelled in both her research work and her teaching. She is fully aware of the efforts and challenges she'll be facing in the future for her career and is deeply committed to succeeding.

I wish you could see Marie now. She's found her gift and

she's sharing it with the world. She's a new person. She has the confidence and the fire and the beauty that comes from doing what she loves. She has, through her journey, made a deep connection with her true self. She has found her purpose and developed a plan for making the contribution she only dreamed of before.

And Joe? Although Joe had been thinking of cutting back even more, with an eye to retiring, he was willing to become the sole breadwinner in the interim. But ultimately Joe not only became motivated to make more money to support them but also found a new level of enthusiasm for his work. With Marie's encouragement and some business coaching, he tapped into a deep level of his own creativity: He has invented, developed, built, and marketed a new device for the aerospace industry that will help secure their financial future.

Several years ago Marie was standing on a precipice. She—and Joe—could have chosen to remain there—surviving, at times mildly happy, but eventually living a life of quiet desperation. Instead she decided to take a daring leap into the unknown. Now she's soaring.

I asked Marie recently, with all her years in the corporate world and now her six years in academia, what she felt was the one thing that complicated people's lives above all others. Without hesitation she said, "Not doing the work you love."

If you're not now doing work you love, you probably know the truth of this statement. As we've seen, doing the work you love is not the only way to simplify your work life, but it is a most effective one.

Marie stopped a few years back and looked at the insanity of continuing to spend her time doing work she didn't love. She imagined a better work life for herself and Joe. She changed her belief system and reinvented herself as someone who could support herself doing work she loves. And she didn't let anyone tell her that going back to school to get a Ph.D. at her age was impossible. She followed the long-held wish of her heart, and she took the leap.

If you're on the verge of making a change in your work life so you can do the work you love, don't wait another day. You'll be amazed at what magically comes to your aid when you take that leap.

85. If Not Now, When?

One of the main concerns Marie had when she was trying to decide whether to take the leap and go for her doctorate was that she was too old. I pointed out that I hadn't written my first book until I was forty-five. Julia Child didn't make her first television appearance until she was fifty-five. Thomas Edison didn't discover electricity until he was fifty-nine. Eleanor Roosevelt didn't become a delegate to the United Nations until she was sixty. And, as it turned out, even Marie's own husband, Joe, didn't do his most creative engineering until he was sixty-two.

But even if we didn't have these and a zillion other examples of people who reached their full stride after what we used to think of as middle age, what's to be gained by waiting? If you don't do it now, when will you do it? Do you want to wait another five years and then start finding work you love? Would you have the energy, the drive, or the impetus to do it then? If you start now you could be well ensconced in your new profession in five or three or two years or less. Do you want to look back when you're forty, fifty, sixty, or seventy and say, "If only I'd started back then I could be finished by now"? And in the meantime, do you really want to spend the rest of your life doing what you're doing now? Do you want to spend even another year doing it? Another six months? Another day?

We don't know if we're going to be around five or ten years from now. Would you want to depart this life without ever having tried to do that challenging task that your soul is calling you to do? Whatever you do, don't let fear or inertia stop you. There's no time like the present to get started.

ACKNOWLEDGMENTS

I want to thank the following people, who contributed immeasurably to this book:

Catha Paquette for her loving and supportive friendship and her ability to wield a killer editing pencil.

Carla Aiello for her ceaseless dedication to helping me become proficient at getting out of computer crashes and her unstinting technical genius when I couldn't do it myself.

Catherine Whitney for rescuing me with her extraordinary writing, editing, and research capabilities.

Philip McKenna and Mike Nichols for the financial planning and tax preparing expertise they graciously shared with me.

Pat Rushton and Joe Phillips for their readiness to step in at a moment's notice and save the day.

Barry Lang for his powerful and healing energy work.

Suzanne Lahl for her intuitive and insightful inner guidance.

Jane Dystel for her friendship and invaluable help as my literary agent.

My publisher Bob Miller at Hyperion, and his wonderful crew, Martha Levin, Jennifer Landers, Ellen Archer, Phil Rose, Lauren Weinberg, Adrian James, and, most especially, my terrific editor, Jennifer Lang.

My former husband, Wolcott Gibbs, Jr., for his continued guidance, love, and support.

My Ecstatic Women's Circle—Lynn, Katherine, Pat, Carol, Elizabeth, Simone, Valerie, Tara, and Divy—for helping me hold the vision; and all the members of the Ecstatic Women's Choir for helping me sing it.

I'd also like to thank Elizabeth Andersen at Universal Press Syndicate for the hawkeye and marvelous sense of humor she brings to her work on my weekly column, and Patricia Rice at Andrews McMeel Publishing for her great care and dedication to the little books.

And I'm grateful to Dan Strutzel, Dave Kuenstle, Shiela Gorman, and Sarah Pond for making my experience with Nightingale Conant such an delightful one.

And most of all I'd like to thank my readers, whose loving and supportive letters add immensely to the joy in my life.

BESTSELLING TITLES
from
ELAINE ST.JAMES

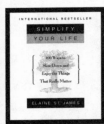

SIMPLIFY YOUR LIFE
100 Ways to Slow Down and Enjoy the Things That Really Matter

If you're overpowered, overextended, and overwhelmed by today's go-go lifestyle, this is your antidote, providing one hundred practical steps for creating a simple and satisfying way of life.

0-7868-8000-7 ● $9.95 (pb)

INNER SIMPLICITY
100 Ways to Regain Peace and Nourish Your Soul

Elaine St. James takes the same principles from *Simplify Your Life* and applies them to our inner lives, showing us how to smile, laugh, and cry; how to conquer our fears; and how to develop gratitude and get comfortable with change.

0-7868-8097-X ● $9.95 (pb)

LIVING THE SIMPLE LIFE
A Guide to Scaling Down and Enjoying More

Eliminate clutter, change your consumer habits, and learn to say no in this blueprint that will: give you more time for play and relaxation, make you more productive, and help you unleash your creativity.

0-7868-8242-5 ● $9.95 (pb)

www.HyperionBooks.com

HYPERION

Get your simplicity to go!

Simplify Your Life
Audiocassette series
From Nightingale-Conant

Overwhelmed by your possessions, finances, commitments, obligations . . . the sheer amount of *stuff* in your life? Then you'll find this practical, entertaining audio program a source of blessed relief. In it Elaine St. James delivers dozens of new ideas, suggestions, and strategies to help you eliminate clutter, simplify household routines, shave hours off your workweek, and reduce expenses while creating more time for the things you enjoy. And the convenient audio format means you can listen while you commute, work, cook, exercise—anytime you can use a Walkman or plug in a tape player. What could be simpler?

To order the *Simplify Your Life* audiocassette series, call us toll-free at 1-800-525-9000. Or visit us on the Web at www.nightingale.com. All orders are backed by our unconditional 30-day money-back guarantee.